The Struggling Entrepreneur

Less Push, More Flow

CHRIS PEARSE

Copyright © 2024 Chris Pearse

All rights reserved.

ISBN: 9798812024475

DEDICATION

This book is dedicated to you, the entrepreneur,
who seeks to give form to your thoughts
And make your dreams come true.

Abracadabra

ACKNOWLEDGEMENTS

I acknowledge with sincere thanks the many entrepreneurs who have enabled me to better understand the dynamics of entrepreneurial activity.

A big thank you also to Chris Lamb, Alex Rocha and Ian Thwaites, who provided invaluable feedback on the draft manuscript.

Much gratitude also goes to Professor John Leonard of the University of Western Ontario, distinguished scholar of John Milton, for shedding light on the Garden of Eden myth.

CONTENTS

DEDICATION	ii
ACKNOWLEDGEMENTS	iii
CONTENTS	iv
INTRODUCTION	1
SO YOU THINK YOU'RE AN ENTREPRENEUR	7
Horror Vacui	9
A Mathematical Hiatus	11
Bloody Lucre	15
Faking it to Make it	18
Imposter Syndrome	21
Takeaways	24
AN ANATOMY OF STRUGGLE	27
Flow - The Opposite Of Struggle	30
Heaven And Hell	32
Difference and Separation	35
The Garden Of Eden	37

Takeaways	42
THE MIND GAMES WE PLAY	**45**
Imagination	46
Consciousness	48
Feelings	50
Thinking	53
Mindsets	59
Takeaways	65
LESS PUSH, MORE FLOW	**67**
An Antidote To Struggle	70
The Monkey Grip	72
Pushing for Growth	77
Takeaways	80
THE INNER FLOW OF PURPOSE	**83**
Integrity	88
Resilience	94
Positivity	97
Mindfulness	100
Takeaways	103
THE OUTER FLOW OF VISION	**105**
Mysticism and Magic	108
Culture	111
Delegation	120
Takeaways	125
TIME AND MONEY	**127**
Time and Tide	128

A Persistent Illusion 131
Do What You Want 134
Money Money Money 137
Money Mindsets 139
Takeaways 145

SUCCESS GUARANTEED — 147
In The Beginning 149
The Cloud of Unknowing 155
Causation and Effectuation 158
The Corruption of Purpose 161
Takeaways 163

PRACTICAL INTEGRATION — 165
Feeling Good 168
Getting What You Want 170
What's Your Purpose? 173
Bouncing Back 175
Inspiring Others 176
Last Words 182

APPENDICES — 185
Appendix 1 - Meditation 186
Appendix 2 - Programs 192
Appendix 3 - Resources 195

ABOUT THE AUTHOR — 197
ALSO… — 201

INTRODUCTION

The Struggling Entrepreneur - a companion book to The Broken CEO - dissects the anatomy of struggle, redefines entrepreneurship to include anyone seeking to fulfil a desire (all of us?) and offers a practical approach for transforming struggle into its opposite: flow.

This is an inside job however, less to do with the circumstances we find ourselves in; more to do with the way we respond to them. My focus is an inner one, exploring the inner dynamics of mind, perception, thought and feeling that contribute more to our experience of the world, than the world itself. Or as one pundit put it:

> Go within or go without

The journey inwards needs no preparation or prior knowledge of psychology, philosophy or neuroscience - simply curiosity and an open mind.

But this is not idle navel-gazing - the metaphorical, existential and metaphysical themes that we use to shine a light within, are not ends in themselves. Entrepreneurs do stuff - they make a difference - they impact the world and change the way we live. So for this book to have any value, it must provide feet-on-the-ground, pragmatic, actionable advice for anyone wanting to realise an ambition, whatever its scope and scale.

The Struggling Entrepreneur addresses the dynamics of translating an idea into form - turning a dream or a vision into a physical reality - manifesting an aspiration or a desire.

Yet, this book will not tell you how to set up or run a business. It will not reveal how to pitch your idea, raise funds or design your exit strategy. There are plenty of excellent books that already fulfil those needs. Neither will it tell you how to *push* through the tough times, attempt to motivate you, or tell you how you can do, be or have anything you want, now.

What it does do - through exploring the way we use our mental faculties - is to reveal how much more power we have at our disposal once we get into alignment with the truth of who and what we really are. Insight into these realities generates the inspiration and reveals the knowledge to transform struggle, in order to experience the ease and flow we hanker for.

Modern neuroscience may be conspicuous by its absence - there is no consideration of our amygdalas, dopamine triggers or neuroplasticity. The study of our objective brains is a fascinating one that is continually breaking new ground. However, it can only ever be a reflection of our actual experience and is accessible solely through evermore cutting-edge instrumentation, observing from the outside in.

In comparison, our subjective minds offer 24/7 access to the most sophisticated apparatus known to man - and from within. For that reason, I have relegated the so-called scientific approach in favour of an experiential one, when it serves.

This book is about the journey of transformation from thought to thing, from possibility to actuality. With elegant symmetry, that journey demands not just the development, growth and refinement of the enterprise, but of the entrepreneur themself.

Oddly, the success that every entrepreneur covets is frequently the biggest obstacle of them all, and the first to overcome. Outcome fixation is incompatible with flow - it is the enemy of peace and the soul-mate of struggle. The resolution of every step into good/bad, success/failure sets the entrepreneur on a roller-coaster ride of emotion that will quickly dissipate the reserves of energy and commitment required for the journey.

The antidote is attention to process. Process proceeds - it is the flow itself. Constant judgement of its results simply impedes or even destroys it. Any gardener that has dug up a germinating seed to 'see how it's getting on' will know how counterproductive that can be.

The entrepreneur is a leader. From solopreneurship to global enterprise, leadership is fundamental and manifests as the ability to inspire yourself and others to create what you may not have even thought possible. If you have any doubt over this, think back to your late teens and consider if you ever foresaw the totality of your life today.

I describe inner and outer aspects of leadership that form pillars, without which enterprises (and entrepreneurs) collapse. With these pillars firmly in place, the health of the enterprise becomes less dependent on its vision and the vicissitudes of the market. This is exactly why many experienced venture capitalists and business angels, when investing, will prioritise the quality of the leadership team over their proposition.

The two resources that entrepreneurs frequently obsess over are time and money. According to some, time is money. A clear perspective on these two commodities is critical for the entrepreneur that wants to shift from a state of struggle into one of flow. Flow is intrinsic to both.

Finally, we entertain how exactly this inner perspective translates into outer action. Action without inner clarity leads to chaos; clarity without action leads to stasis. Both are commonly regarded as failures. Yet once a degree of inner clarity is achieved, inaction is not an option - the alignment of thought, feeling and energy promotes flow, and stuff will happen.

Providing clarity of mind is sustained and prioritised over

results, your inner alignment of thought, feeling and energy will allow you to navigate the outer circumstances you encounter with what is commonly called success. In this frame of mind, even a total lack of experience and proficiency will fail to stand in the way of the entrepreneur and their goals.

Clearly all of us have dreams and aspirations, whether or not we call ourselves entrepreneurs. And we all meet impediments to their realisation. The Struggling Entrepreneur's message thus applies to all of us, with or without the profit motive that we associate with entrepreneurial activity.

Nonetheless, my experience of working with hundreds of entrepreneurs has shown me how the need to generate more income than expenditure - to turn a profit - greatly amplifies the challenges, compared to many other non-commercial endeavours.

Everyone craves success - even if some have managed to suppress the urge. Yet not all of us agree on the nature of success. Some want riches, some fame, some achievement and others meaning. Whatever your definition, the *feeling* of success is universal, independently of context. It is no more the birthright of the titans of Silicon Valley, than it is of a hill farmer on a remote Scottish island.

As we'll explore, anyone that sets about making an idea a reality is an entrepreneur - and that includes you and me. Success is found in the fun and enjoyment of the journey, regardless of the destination.

SO YOU THINK YOU'RE AN ENTREPRENEUR

Much has been written about entrepreneurs and entrepreneurship - in particular the business, commercial and financial aspects of it. Investopedia defines it thus:

"An entrepreneur is an individual who creates a new business, bearing most of the risks and enjoying most of the rewards. The process of setting up a business is known as entrepreneurship. The entrepreneur is commonly seen as an innovator, a source of new ideas, goods, services, and business/or procedures."

This certainly aligns with the common conception of an entrepreneur as someone who sees opportunities where others don't and exploits them to financial advantage. But an 'innovator, a source of new ideas, goods...' etc. could just as easily be an engineer. And if you're doubting the need for financial discipline in engineering, Arthur M. Wellington, a 19th century civil engineer was reputed to have said:

"An engineer can do for a dollar what any fool can do for two."

Perhaps we can apply this adage to entrepreneurship?

What about risk? It is undoubtedly true that an entrepreneur who turns her back on a salary to face the uncertainty and volatility of income from a new enterprise is exposed to higher levels of risk than most. Yet the worst-case scenario from a business failure may be comparable to an unexpected redundancy: long-term unemployment.

I'm not for a moment denying that successful entrepreneurs need to face extraordinary circumstances on occasion, simply that risk is present whether or not our activity is 'entrepreneurial'.

Let's take a look at the original meaning of the word entrepreneur. A relatively new word dating from the 19th century, it derives unsurprisingly from the earlier word, enterprise, Old French for undertaking. So an entrepreneur can, in the most general case, be considered an undertaker of some activity.

North American readers may be amused to discover that the British English meaning of undertaker now refers exclusively to a funeral director or mortician. Since the business of funerals is not regarded as particularly entrepreneurial in nature, we can consider the two unrelated, notwithstanding the high mortality rate of new enterprises!

This rather convenient etymology allows me to take the liberty of treating anyone undertaking a project, assignment, mission, job, task or enterprise as an entrepreneur. Anyone, that is, who is intent on turning an idea into a manifest reality.

This, in turn, enables us to explore the transformation of 'thoughts into things' and the challenges that it attracts, which is the central purpose of this book.

Far from attempting to redefine entrepreneurship, embracing the root meaning will allow us to extend our learnings to a broader base.

The Struggling Entrepreneur therefore concerns those who have met challenges on their journeys from idea to actuality. I make no apology if that includes the whole of humanity.

HORROR VACUI

Many times during the writing of this book, I've been painfully aware of a yawning gap between the best-seller lodged firmly in my imagination, and the blank page staring back at me from my laptop. The discrepancy between the two is stark, vivid and occasionally intimidating.

This gap is not just a static void, it is a hiatus, which one dictionary describes as "a space from which something requisite to completeness is absent". Is that familiar? Have you ever had a sense that a space, or indeed a time, needs to be filled, and thus completed, by some action yet to be taken?

I would suggest that you, and every person on the planet, is intimately acquainted with this feeling, being integral to the human experience. Whether you are about to clean your teeth or plan the colonisation of Mars, the basic sequence is identical: firstly you identify a possibility that you desire, and then decide to make it manifest.

This mechanism relies on the disparity between what could be, and what is; between the potential and the 'reality'; between the world of imagination and its physical manifestation. The larger the hiatus, the greater the apparent challenge.

The Greek philosopher and polymath, Aristotle, was reputed to have said: "Horror vacui", which is often translated as nature abhors a vacuum. Suck the air out of an empty beer bottle and it will immediately refill itself - with air, not beer, alas - just as soon as you release it from your lips.

Although Aristotle's assertion was initially contested, modern physics confirms that not only does nature hate vacuums, it forbids them. Ultra-high vacuum chambers can currently reduce pressure to a trillionth of an atmosphere, but still leave around 100 particles per cubic centimetre. The closest physical approximation to an absolute vacuum, intergalactic space, accommodates a few hydrogen atoms per cubic metre. Even if we were able to extract every atom from a closed space, quantum physics dictates that subatomic particles would eventually intrude and banish the perfect vacuum from our physical reality.

Nature's urge to fill 3-dimensional space is powerful enough to make true physical vacuums impossible. The human urge to fill the possibility space with its manifestations, I would argue, is comparably strong - fulfilment is the reward.

The metaphor of a vacuum as the point of inception works at a number of levels, particularly so as a space that can not only contain anything you wish to place in it, but insists on doing so, relentlessly drawing stuff into it.

So the entrepreneur's raison d'être is to identify the vacuum within and allow the right thought, feeling and action to fill the void to her satisfaction, transforming an idea into a manifest reality in the process. Let's see what one example looks like in practice.

A Mathematical Hiatus

Pierre de Fermat was a 17th century French mathematician, credited by Isaac Newton with early work leading to the development of infinitesimal calculus - the mathematics of change. Although his crowning achievement was with the theory of numbers, he is best remembered today for his eponymous last theorem.

Fermat's Last Theorem states that there is no integer solution for the equation:

$$a^n + b^n = c^n$$

If n is greater than 2.

You may recognise that when n = 2, the equation becomes Pythagoras's theorem which defines the relationship between the length of sides of a right-angle triangle:

$$a^2 + b^2 = c^2$$

Fermat affirmed that when you use cubes instead of squares, or any higher power still, there are no three positive integers (whole numbers) that will satisfy this equation.

In the context of pure mathematics, this is a pretty simple theorem to state. Anyone with basic numeracy will grasp it without too much effort. But why this should hold true, and how to prove the conjecture is another matter altogether.

Fermat published the theorem around 1637, noting that he had a proof that was too large to fit in the margins. He died with the proof unpublished.

But Fermat did not just state a theorem, he created a vacuum - a hiatus of knowledge and understanding. He created a space that was yearning to be filled.

The following centuries saw Fermat's theorem attract more failed proofs than any other in the history of mathematics, in a frenzied attempt to fill the void of knowledge. Its challenge drew cash prizes and the promise of glory and fame beyond the confines of mathematics.

In 1963, a young English schoolboy stumbled across Fermat's theorem. Fascinated by the existence of a hypothesis that was so easy to state that he, a ten-year-old, could understand, but that no one had proven, he decided to be the first person to conquer the challenge.

In 1995, Andrew Wiles, now a professor of mathematics, published his completed proof of Fermat's last theorem, some 32 years after first becoming aware of it. Just like nature, Wiles wanted to fill the vacuum that Fermat had bequeathed.

However, unlike the momentary rush of air that refills the empty beer bottle, and the satisfying pop that goes with it, Wiles needed time to grapple with a problem that many eminent mathematicians declared impossible to solve after 350 years of failed attempts. He did so in near total secrecy, only going public in June 1993.

In August of the same year, a flaw was discovered. In trying to rectify it, Wiles nearly gave up, but just at the point of capitulation, a year later, Wiles found a way of circumventing the flaw altogether and soon after, published the final proof that Fermat's theorem was true.

In Wiles' proof of the veracity of Fermat's theorem, we have an example of the kind of intensity, tenacity and single-minded focus that can be required to transform an imagined outcome into a manifest one (Simon Singh provides more detail in his excellent book: Fermat's Last Theorem). This is work in its broadest sense, and it lies behind every human endeavour that has been undertaken, from peeling an orange to decoding the human genome.

For those keen to attach a profit motive to entrepreneurship, Wiles won significant sums of money as a direct result of his breakthrough. His reputed net worth is rather more than one might associate with a professor of mathematics, no doubt boosted by the fame his work drew, not just the prize money.

But why did Wiles dedicate a large chunk of his career to this enterprise? Was it for the money? Was it for the fame? Or was it simply "because it's there" - the reply George Leigh Mallory used when he was asked why he wanted to climb Mount Everest.

Certainly, there are many financially successful entrepreneurs, operating in commercial markets, that don't cite money as the driving incentive, whilst openly appreciating the freedom it gives them. Apple founder, Steve Jobs, declared "I never did it for the money". As a somewhat less successful engineer myself, I can vouch for the thrill of designing and developing new digital systems being far more exciting and life-enhancing than any monetary recompense.

Without any doubt, money is necessary - but, for the entrepreneur, it is far from sufficient.

Fame, not just fortune, accompany the few entrepreneurs that succeed at scale, but neither are sustainable without the radical transformations that they bring about in their fields of expertise. From Ford to Musk, from Carnegie to Gates - each has revolutionised their spheres of activity, paving the way for massive technological and societal shifts.

When we observe world-class entrepreneurs, we often perceive the wealth and renown ahead of the wider impact they have had. Our media systematically promotes the tangible rewards that successful entrepreneurs reap, ahead of the benefits to society. Yet when the individual prioritises the personal trappings of success, things can easily unravel, occasionally in spectacular fashion.

BLOODY LUCRE

At the peak of her success, Elizabeth Holmes was lauded as the youngest, female, self-made billionaire in history - the next Steve Jobs. She had succeeded in raising $700m for her company, Theranos, which was valued at $9bn. Investors included Rupert Murdoch of News Corp, Larry Ellison of Oracle and the Walton family behind Walmart.

Her goal was to build a portable device that would apply 200+ tests to a small vial of blood taken from a pin prick rather than inserting a needle into a vein. The benefits were clear - lower cost, faster turnaround, less blood, greater accessibility and earlier detection of disease.

The mission statement was: "To facilitate the early detection and prevention of disease and empower people everywhere to live their best possible lives." A compelling vision indeed -

one which allied to her charisma, passion and communication skills enabled her to attract and convince interest at the highest levels. Her board of directors included three ex-secretaries of state, Henry Kissinger and George Schultz amongst them.

Holmes gave every impression of being a dyed-in-the-wool entrepreneur. She dropped out of college at age 19 to pursue her dream. She wore black turtle-necks like Steve Jobs. She named her machine the Edison: "because we assumed we'd have to fail 10,000 times to get it to work the ten-thousand-and-first. And we did." By her own admission: "I work all the time, and I'm basically in the office from the time I wake up and then working until I go to sleep every day."

The commitment and focus were exemplary. She also demonstrated superhuman degrees of resilience, never taking no for an answer (sacking the naysayers instead) and refusing to allow any failure to block her progress towards ultimate triumph and glory. Her deep voice (some say affected) and concise, articulate speech amplified her credibility for many.

Everyone who met her was left in no doubt that she had what it took and was of the right stuff to achieve her vision.

The combination of intense drive and determination was always going to ensure that Holmes made a significant impact on the world. The problem was that however necessary these attributes are, they will never be sufficient to succeed as an entrepreneur.

In 2023, Holmes started an 11 year prison sentence for fraud.

The Edison had failed to deliver reliable results, so Holmes touted results from commercial blood test laboratories as her own, presumably in an attempt to buy time for further development work.

Her obsession with dismissing any failure that could detract from the impression of inexorable progress required tight, internal security and a ferocious legal team led by another Theranos board member, David Boies. Having a reputation for 'destroying' opponents on the witness stand (including Bill Clinton), Boies was known and feared in equal measure.

Tyler Schultz, a Theranos engineer, was witnessing the deception on a daily basis. He speaks of how the charismatic Holmes could easily lift his spirits after a string of technical failures, but he could not live with the ongoing deceit that was taking place. His grandfather and board member, George Schultz, sided with Holmes and advised him not to speak out. When he eventually did, he was landed with a $400,000 legal bill defending himself against David Boies' firm. His parents considered selling their house to cover the sum.

So what went wrong for Elizabeth Holmes? How did her extraordinary entrepreneurship degenerate so spectacularly and finally turn against her? How did such a brilliant young woman, hailed by the great and the good, fall into the depths of criminal disgrace?

Clearly, this has nothing to do with the viability of her vision. We can cite many reasons why either the project was never technologically possible, or how its development was mismanaged. Neither matter one jot. The issue centres on Holmes' transition from optimistic trier, to cynical cheat.

The answer to these questions, in my view, lie in the lack of congruence between Holmes' vision and her purpose. We'll be exploring these key elements of entrepreneurship later on. For now I would suggest that a lack of alignment between the two compromised her integrity and accelerated her degeneration.

Faking it to Make it

One of the mottos frequently touted by the entrepreneurial community is:

> Fake it to make it

The formula draws as much derision from other quarters as it does support from its advocates. The very idea of faking anything is plainly a sign of a breached integrity, moral decrepitude even. Surely fakery is a hollow pretence at best - treachery at worst? As true as this may be, I would argue that without a degree of 'fakery', no human will ever reach potential, entrepreneurs in particular.

Cast your mind back to learning how to ride a bicycle for the first time. You've seen people on bicycles before, seemingly defy gravity by maintaining balance on an intrinsically unstable platform - and get from a to b faster than you can run! It all looks so easy, you know you can do it too. You are already a cyclist in your mind - you may even have experienced cycling at breakneck speed in your imagination, if not yet in reality.

Then you get on the bike, start pedalling and immediately fall off. You dust yourself down and get straight back on, only to fall off again, and again, and again. By this time the gap between what you have imagined and what you have accomplished is wider than ever. The evidence from your experience says you just can't do it, but the imagination knows you can. You know that if you can keep pretending for just long enough, you will succeed in manifesting what is currently limited to your imagination. From the moment you climb on the bike to the point at which you can ride it, you are a fake, faking it to make it.

Of course there are examples of others who have filled this void before you, but what about the first person to ever ride a bicycle? And just because someone else can do it doesn't make your success a certitude. By this token, all learners are fakers and so are all entrepreneurs.

Richard Branson, a global paragon of entrepreneurialism, is quite clear that: "If someone offers you an opportunity, whether you know anything about it or not, say yes and then go and learn how to do it. Life's a lot more fun that way."

Over the course of my career, on numerous occasions, I've been asked if I would take on projects that have been completely outside my area of expertise and comfort. On each occasion, my ability to deliver has been in real doubt - at least to me - with no track record of a similar achievement to bolster my confidence. Yet, instead of admitting to real doubts over my competence to complete the task, I would always take it on, affirming a successful outcome.

The key criterion was never "Can I do this?" but "Do I want to do it?"

Some might level a charge of arrogance against this kind of entrepreneurial spirit. In the original sense of the word, they would be correct: *arrogare* meaning "to claim for oneself, assume."

The entrepreneur needs to willingly enter a realm in which their dream is as much a reality in their imagination, as it is a delusion in the world of matter. The first step frequently being in opposition to the collective opinions of those around them. The journey they embark on is the hero's journey marked by a series of challenges both physical and psychological which compel the hero - in our case, the entrepreneur - to transform at a personal level. Only through accelerated personal evolution can the hero rise to the challenge and overcome it - before being presented with a series of greater ones.

The process seems designed to confront the hero with as much doubt as they can endure by presenting them with the largest possible disparity between dream and reality: their imagination within them, and the world of appearances around them.

Only someone with the conviction that they can do what

their senses (and others) tell them they can't, will succeed. The act of faking seems implicit in any undertaking that requires the individual to achieve against the odds.

Those of us who are willing to break boundaries (generally our own, if not those of others) will, sooner or later, meet with the idea that maybe we just aren't up to the task and are likely to get found out. Not only are we fakers, but imposters, to boot.

IMPOSTER SYNDROME

Howard Schultz, the three times CEO of Starbucks, has admitted to feeling both undeserving and insecure, despite successfully leading a major global corporation. In a New York Times interview, Schultz confessed, "Very few people, whether you've been in that job before or not, get into the seat and believe that today they are now qualified to be the CEO. They're not going to tell you that, but it's true."

This is an example of Imposter Syndrome in which the sufferer repeatedly entertains the possibility that they are not qualified or competent to execute the responsibilities they've signed up for. They carry a fear that their inadequacies will be unveiled at any moment, exposing them as charlatans, frauds and fakes.

I've worked with many senior leaders that have admitted to this syndrome. Not one of them has demonstrated - to me at least - any degree of incompetence that would preclude them from the position they hold.

Yet, in marked contrast, those few who have displayed serious shortcomings in their professional abilities have been quite incapable of recognising the fact, let alone addressing it. When challenged, it is as if they simply could not countenance any flaw at all. This is a feature of narcissism which seems to insulate the sufferer from all external criticism and internal insecurity, rendering change unlikely, if not impossible.

Imposters, on the other hand, respond well to the following insights:

Firstly, the revelation that the fear of being outed as an imposter is perfectly normal. It is far more common than many 'imposters' realise - my observation being that it is part and parcel of being a functioning human.

Secondly, the alternative to feeling like an imposter is that of feeling beyond any judgement, including one's own. This is a trait of narcissism. Would you prefer to be a narcissist or an imposter?

Thirdly, the original meaning of imposter is simply someone that 'puts in place'. No sense of fraud or deceit there. In fact, it is the essence of entrepreneurial activity.

Finally, as in any process of learning or development such as riding a bicycle, there has to be a phase in which you are 'pretending' that you know what you are doing - making it up as you go along. If you remove the 'fakery' of the imposter from human activity, you erase any possibility of growth, development and entrepreneurism.

So, far from decrying or attempting to cure imposter syndrome, it needs acknowledging, embracing and celebrating. The alternative is a narcissistic arrogance which can border on the psychopathic.

Entrepreneurs are imposters and fakers par excellence.

But, where is the line between the fakery of learning to ride a bike and that of Elizabeth Holmes, the fraud? The outcomes are clear: one gets you from a to b, whilst the other gets you straight to prison. The real difference, however, can be found in the intention and, in particular, the purpose behind the actions.

Purpose is central to all entrepreneurial activity. Without it, the resolve and energy to work through the inevitable obstacles en route will not be available. But purpose is not enough - it needs to be expressed through a vision, with which it is fully aligned. When purpose and vision are not congruent, integrity is undermined, opening the gates to practices that harm the enterprise, those involved in it, and the entrepreneur themself.

Takeaways

- We are all entrepreneurs, filling the void of opportunity and possibility

- Our mission is to give physical form to imagination

- Money is always a means, never an end

- Entrepreneurs need to fake it, if only to themselves

- Imposter syndrome is natural to good entrepreneurs

- Integrity lies in the alignment between purpose and vision

AN ANATOMY OF STRUGGLE

When I was a child, duvets were an exotic Swedish phenomenon that the entrepreneur and founder of Habitat, Sir Terence Conran, introduced to the UK. They caught on very rapidly thanks to the advantage of being able to make your bed in a few seconds. In spite of this and numerous other benefits, my mother steadfastly refused to adopt the trend, preferring sheets, blankets, bedspreads and hospital corners (a method of bed-making using overlapping folds in the sheet that are less likely to come loose).

The sensation of being tightly cocooned inside these warm layers was generally comforting and particularly welcome in winter when ice would form inside, as well as outside, the windows. But on several occasions the bed would resemble more of a living coffin as I would wake up to find myself upside down with my head where my feet should be.

The combination of sleep paralysis, narrow bed and those damned hospital corners meant that no amount of struggle could set me free. I can recall the feelings of claustrophobia and terror at the prospect of never being able to get out of my warm tomb. Even now, the recollection is deeply uncomfortable.

That feeling of being tightly bound in a straitjacket, unable to free oneself, is a defining element of struggle. But, as we will explore, it is not the only one.

Compare this physical example of struggle with the analogous emotional one of Franz Kafka's Description of a Struggle, in which he portrays how the individual can struggle against social norms. If Kafka intended the struggle to extend to the reader, he succeeded! This stifling of the ability to express oneself is at the heart of the experience of struggle.

Expression is a fundamental human urge. To express is to press, push or squeeze out words and actions from oneself in such a way as to impact the world around us. In terms of our previous metaphor, it is the ability to fill a vacuum.

Struggle denotes difficulty, stubbornness and resistance. Nothing new there. The laws of physics tell us that to do any work, there has to be resistance. In terms of pulling a load over a distance, the work done is equal to the force required to overcome any resistance, multiplied by the distance travelled.

$$\text{Work} = \text{Force} \times \text{Distance}$$

If the resistance is too much to overcome and no movement takes place, then no work is done, regardless of the force applied. If the load is moved on bearings offering no resistance at all, no work is done either - even though the load has moved.

The same holds true for the entrepreneur - too much resistance and the enterprise won't flourish; too little and it will hold no interest for an entrepreneurial spirit.

Yet struggle is not just overcoming resistance. According to W. W. Skeat's etymological dictionary, the word is related to Scandinavian words for ill-will, strife, dispute and contention. Online definitions include "forceful or violent efforts to get free of restraint or constriction". There is a clear, emotionally-charged aspect to struggle, which includes the possibility that not only could the struggle be unsuccessful, but that it could overwhelm and even crush the struggler in the process.

Struggle implies that you are bound, constrained and held back from doing what you want to do. You are not free. The efforts you make appear futile - the load you are heaving doesn't move. And without movement - regardless of the force deployed - no work is done. There is no impact, no progress.

You are almost certainly acquainted with the corresponding emotions: frustration at having one's free will thwarted; anger at the circumstances and people that appear to hinder you; impotence from your inability to make the impact you want; and finally fear - and even possibly shame - that you could remain permanently inferior to the challenges you face, doomed to failure.

The manifestations of struggle are as varied as those who experience them, from being trapped upside down in bed, to trying to make financial ends meet - from being denied expression, to scrabbling for elusive sales. But the accompanying emotions are not so dissimilar.

FLOW - THE OPPOSITE OF STRUGGLE

We are well-acquainted with the potent cocktail of these emotions. But, paradoxically perhaps, we also feel intimately familiar with their antitheses: ease, flow, fulfilment, satisfaction, serenity, power and clarity. Even if we can't remember the last time, or any time that we felt these, I suggest we all know exactly how they feel.

So how is it that we can find ourselves drowning in a maelstrom of pain and negativity when we all carry such a clear familiarity with, and desire for its opposite? How can it be that we find ourselves in a state which is the very opposite to the one we know and crave?

These two states of feeling, and the gulf between them, seem to emerge from the difference between the circumstances we desire and those that appear to prevail - another form of vacuum. Our belief being that fulfilling our quest to manifest our dream will transform the emotional hell of struggle, into a paradise of achievement.

A possibly controversial premise of this book is that the way we feel is not a result of the circumstances we find ourselves in. In reality the contrary is true - our outer circumstances reflect back to us the thoughts and feelings we give life to in our minds. The causal relationship we see between them - that our feelings are at the mercy of circumstance - is a self-created illusion. Further, the more we attribute the way we feel to the world we experience, the more adversarial the world appears and the greater the struggle it seems to present us with.

That being the case, the antidote to struggle lies not in what we do, so much as what and how we perceive, the thoughts we entertain, the stories we tell ourselves and the feelings that they evoke - all of which are at our command.

Have you ever noticed how the relief of struggle through the attainment of a goal can be very short-lived? Before you know it, the struggle reappears in another form and a different context, seemingly in order to demonstrate beyond doubt that the challenge and the struggle are, in truth, unrelated.

More clear evidence arises when we compare two similarly able people in comparable circumstances, where one thrives and excels, whilst the other struggles to make any progress. At its nadir, the experience is, figuratively at least, hellish. At its zenith, heavenly.

HEAVEN AND HELL

Heaven and hell are apt metaphors for the experience of flow and struggle respectively. We do not have to wait until the end of our earthly adventure to experience either. They are both accessible at every moment of our human lives and subject to individual choice. Clearly, no one in their right minds would consciously choose to experience hell on earth. The experience of heaven on earth is effectively choiceless - but only when one's consciousness permits a true perspective of reality.

Between these two extremes lies a spectrum of experience which, I suspect, we have all encountered at some stage of our lives, however fleetingly. Dante Alighieri wrote extensively about these levels of experience in his Divine Comedy, albeit post mortem experiences. The levels are characterised in terms of sin and virtue - some of which we may not be personally acquainted with. Hopefully, heresy, violence, fraud and treachery will feel quite alien to most.

A different and more familiar way of labelling the steps on this stairway to heaven might be to describe the way we feel at each point of ascension or descension.

In 1995, Dr. David R. Hawkins published his Map of Consciousness which describes a scale of emotions ranging from shame and humiliation at the bottom, to peace and bliss at the top. These are likely more relatable and accessible to us than Dante's circles of heaven, purgatory and hell. The eight lowest emotions are as follows:

Shame represents the very lowest emotional state, in which the humiliated would wish away their very existence and cease to be. This is rock bottom - the only way is up.

Guilt follows shame, in which the guilty blame themselves, supported by those around them. This represents a marginally higher state because guilt seeks redemption, not oblivion.

Apathy ensues, bringing a sense of hopelessness, but lacking the self-condemnation of guilt and shame.

Grief brings a sense of regret at the loss of something or someone. It represents an inflexion point on the scale as the individual starts to look beyond their own limited existence to that of others.

Fear acknowledges influences beyond the control of the individual. It is, to a degree, outward looking but chronic anxiety eventually forces withdrawal from the world.

Desire - a craving or yearning - derives from a sense of lack or limitation, a feeling of incompleteness, another sign of extraversion.

Anger is often the active face of fear, condemning whatever is wrong with the situation or relationship and compelling its resolution by force, violence if necessary. Anger fuels not just the judgement of others, but also the reaction to it.

Pride is at the top of this scale of negative emotions. The

proud value themselves, but may still judge and censure others, even without voicing the judgement.

These eight emotions, when felt with a certain intensity, can be collectively described as living in hell. Struggle is implicit to all of them, with the possible exception of shame. Even apathy will generate struggle when it comes to fulfilling the basics of staying alive.

Scratching below the surface of all these states reveals a common factor. Without judgement not one of these feelings can survive. Judgement cannot take place without comparison. So, at the root of all these manifestations of living hell lies the act of comparing yourself with something other, that is separate from and not part of you.

We can deduce from this that the root cause of struggle is the habitual comparison of yourself with something other than you. That other can be real or an idealised image, it makes no difference. In essence, it's trying to be what you believe you are not.

There are two possible responses to this paradigm, other than submitting to it. We can push, shove and strain against the apparent reality in order to force it to comply with our desires. Or we can change the belief system behind the reality:

> Everything I want to be, I already am.

However irrational that may sound, it repositions you away from the lack and limitation that you may be struggling against. It becomes an antidote to the constant inner refrain: I am not what/where/who I want to be. I am not enough.

It also reflects how potentiality and reality are not separate. Reality is contained within potentiality just as a complete human being is contained within its single-celled embryo - the zygote.

The process of growth and development, therefore, is not so much becoming something new, but rather uncovering, or remembering that which you are. Looked at in a different way, how could you aspire to be something you are not already well-acquainted with?

DIFFERENCE AND SEPARATION

There are two ways we can relate to the world around us. We can perceive it as separate and different, or we can live in the awareness of the interconnectedness of all things. We can see a tree as a discrete and separate entity - one that is entirely different from, and unconnected to a human being - or we can perceive it as the other half of our lungs, converting the carbon dioxide we exhale into the oxygen we inhale. The former claims independence, the latter embraces symbiosis.

That there is a vast variation in the natural world is beyond dispute. At one level we are entirely different from other species. At another, we are all one within the biosphere - a heaving mass of interdependency.

How we relate to the variety of form around us determines the quality of our lives. The more difference and separation we perceive, the more struggle we experience. Let's consider the perception of difference, and its consequences, as a spectrum:

Destruction: at the very lowest level, there is no commonality with anything different - it appears as a threat and demands destruction. Anyone challenging this 'fact' also deserves annihilation. Socrates, Jesus, Martin Luther King and many others have met this fate.

Conflict: one step removed from destruction, conflict maintains the antagonism towards difference but falls short of resolving it through destruction. Football tribalism, political allegiances and workplace bullying are all examples.

Tolerance: the neutral ground between love and hate, tolerance can be indifferent, but it can also be a mask of acceptability, behind which the antipathy festers. Working relationships often default to this state, allowing colleagues to 'rub along' without discernible animosity.

Respect: literally meaning to look back at, respect begins to value difference. In the looking back, we see commonality, not just contrast. We see something in others that we see in ourselves, which is the beginning of unity.

Love: when alikeness overwhelms and difference is celebrated. Note how the word like, meaning not different, is also a partial synonym for love.

Beyond these familiar states of being, there are two more that are worthy of mention:

Imagination: in which the apparent differences between imagination and reality are perceived as illusory. Imagination is known to be the progenitor of form, and with the right incubation, thoughts must become things.

Pure Consciousness: an agenda-less and timeless state of pure being, beyond any human concept of difference.

These last two states are not in everyone's experience and are offered as possibilities to explore. They are well-documented in eastern and western esoteric teachings.

THE GARDEN OF EDEN

The Bible's book of Genesis describes how Adam and Eve are expelled from Paradise as a consequence of eating the fruit of the Tree of Knowledge of Good and Evil. The myth contains some important features of the human psyche that are central to the experience of struggle and its relief.

As with many myths, the core wisdom is encoded in metaphor and analogy. This is said to hide it from the uninitiated and protect it from the profane, whilst revealing new meaning to those ready to receive it. This use of metaphor also makes the esoteric accessible by using the everyday to represent the abstract.

Before we attempt to expose any messages hidden within the myth, we need to draw attention to certain critical details that are easily missed:

Firstly, the action takes place in the Garden of Eden - also known as Paradise. Both of these names refer to an earthly realm, not a heavenly one. The origin of Paradise derives from the ancient Iranian word for park or enclosure.

Secondly, the forbidden fruit that Adam and Eve bite into, comes from the Tree of Knowledge of Good and Evil. This is often abbreviated to, and understood as just the Tree of Knowledge - a crucial mistake.

When Adam and Eve eat the fruit, they absorb what the tree stands for. The essence of the tree becomes a part of them. That essence is the knowledge of good and evil. This knowledge is quite specific - it allows you to discriminate between things that are good and those that are not. It is the faculty of judgement which splits the world of experience into two camps - good and bad.

This is a polarisation - a separation - which forces you to take sides. Suddenly everything on your side of the fence becomes worthy of your love and respect. Everything else suffers rejection and exclusion. It is a human faculty that creates duality and division.

As I write, many aspects of life are immersed in a binary polarisation ranging from American politics to the transgender debate; from vaccines to cancel culture. Yet it is not the ideological positions that are problematic - they, like any construct, are neutral. It is the identification with them and the separation that they generate between us, as a result, that create a hell on earth for those most entrenched in them.

In contrast, free from judgement, the world takes on a very different feel. The interdependence of all things - represented by the Tree of Life - becomes conspicuous. Although less prominent in the biblical myth, the Tree of Life is a universal symbol, found in many disparate cultures, representing the interconnectedness of the entire creation.

Without judgement, harmony displaces discord and the hell of separation is deposed by a paradise in which the underlying unity in all things is known without shadow of doubt.

We all have personal experience of this state and we can witness it in any child before a certain age (around seven years) at which the faculty of judgement becomes active.

Shakespeare's Hamlet puts it succinctly: "Why then 'tis none to you; for there is nothing either good or bad, but thinking makes it so."

The thinking in Hamlet's quote is the act of judging and labelling. Before the fruit was consumed, there was ignorance of this knowledge and, as we know all too well, ignorance can be bliss.

When we judge anything, we pass sentence on it, just like the judge presiding in a court of law. The sentence is along the lines of: I don't like this - it is bad (evil). In isolation, this sequence of events is innocuous, the problem being that all thoughts create attendant feelings. Thoughts and feelings are like two sides of the same coin, or two poles of a magnet - they cannot be separated. So having passed sentence with a thought, you are compelled (by psychological law) to experience the feeling that goes with it. Negative thoughts create negative feelings, and so you are condemned to experience the negative feeling that a negative thought creates.

In other words, you pass the same sentence on yourself that you pass on others.

This is how a simple act of judgement can instantly remove you from a blissful experience of heaven on earth and dump you into a state of abject misery - a hell on earth.

The myth uses nakedness - the ultimate expression of lack - to signify the impact of the 'fall'. Yet notice how the couple were already naked in their state of paradisiacal bliss, so nothing changed other than their perception, brought about solely by their newly found faculty of judgement. The lack of clothing caused them to feel shame - the lowest of all the human emotions.

Thereafter, the couple are condemned to live in exile and guaranteed a much more difficult existence than that afforded by paradise - a struggle, in fact.

So, judgement creates struggle - that is the central theme of this eisegesis. But if we were to withdraw the power of judgement from our psyches, we would be left unable to survive in the world we live in, relegated to animal status. The answer to this conundrum lies simply in the degree to which we identify with the judgements we make - how much we invest ourselves in the sentences we pass. Or, in other words, how much we mind the experiences we meet.

At the start of the 1962 film Lawrence of Arabia, T. E. Lawrence (played by Peter O'Toole) lights a match and uses his fingers to extinguish it. When Corporal Potter tries the same trick he exclaims "Ooh, it damn well hurts!". "Of course it hurts." replies Lawrence. "So what's the trick, then?" asks the corporal. "The trick, William Potter, is not minding that it hurts."

Minding in this sense is the act of deploying judgement - a faculty of mind - and concluding that pain and suffering are synonymous: pain is bad. Lawrence is able to separate the two as does the Indian mystic and author, Sadhguru:

"Pain is just there in the body. Suffering is something that you create. But you need not create it. If you are aware, you will not create suffering for yourself. The only reason why anyone would create suffering for himself is because he is unaware. Would you create suffering for yourself intentionally? No."

The more we mind life, the more of a struggle it becomes. This is why humour is such a good antidote for the experience of struggle - you cannot mind something you laugh at. Judgement is implicit in minding - a light-hearted approach is its antithesis.

These two states are mutually exclusive - you cannot drag one into the other. Judgement and your identification with it, must be abandoned to transcend struggle and experience flow.

Takeaways

- Struggle is experienced as the resistance to expression
- Flow and struggle mirror heaven and hell
- Struggle is the consequence of comparison
- You already are what you want to be
- Judgement begets struggle
- Humour is an antidote to minding

THE MIND GAMES WE PLAY

It's all in the mind is a familiar cliché, frequently used to suggest that something is the product of the human imagination and therefore has no basis in reality. You may remember your parents suggesting to you that your sense of feeling unwell was self-created and that you would feel fine again once you were out of bed and in school.

They had a point - we must all have experienced the shift in feeling that accompanies a change in thinking. If your best friend had come round to play when you were feeling under the weather, the barrier to getting up would undoubtedly have been lowered.

So, does that prove beyond doubt that the world of the imagination, having less substance and density than the physical world around us, is less real and thus less significant? This is an assumption that goes unchallenged for many of us, reinforced every time an external event appears to wholly determine our thinking and feeling.

IMAGINATION

William Blake, the visionary romantic, said: "Imagination is the real and eternal world of which this vegetable universe is but a faint shadow."

Albert Einstein said: "Imagination is more important than knowledge. Knowledge is limited. Imagination encircles the world."

Neville Goddard, the New Thought author and mystic said: "Determined imagination, thinking from the end, is the beginning of all miracles."

"Imagination is the life force of genius" is sometimes attributed to Nikola Tesla, an undisputed genius himself.

Your imagination is the birthplace of your ideas, thoughts and beliefs. Without the human imagination none of the artefacts around you would exist, from the kitchen sink to your Apple watch. Their origins are all found in the minds of one or more people, developed across the generations. One might say that the imagination is the cause, and the physical manifestation, the effect.

Now, a cause can exist without its effect - you can imagine something without it becoming a physical reality - but an effect can never exist without its cause. The car on your drive could not exist in time and space without an imagination having conceived and given birth to it.

This begs a critical question: Which is more real, cause or effect?

Which, in turn, requires an explanation of the word real. A revealing mediaeval Latin meaning is: "belonging to the thing itself". Whether or not a cause can belong to itself, an effect cannot belong to itself, being inextricably entangled with its cause. So by this admittedly stretched, but plausible logic, a cause is more real than an effect. Which brings us to the counterintuitive conclusion:

> An idea is more real than its physical actuality.

By that token, our minds are more real - or, at the very least, just as real - as the world out there. And this makes more sense when you consider that everything we perceive going on around us, is only and always perceived within us. In reality, there is no 'out there' - everything is played out in the theatre of our minds.

Let that possibility sit with you a while - suspend all judgement and engage your curiosity. Could it be so? And if it is, what are the implications? How would it impact your perception of reality?

The purpose here is not to convince you of anything, merely to question a conclusion that many of us reach without testing - that our outer world rules over our inner world, that we are victims of circumstance. Challenging this paves the way to freeing us from the hegemony of circumstance over our lives, to reestablish the possibility of true free-will, self-determination and the power to create the outcomes we want.

This is the essence of entrepreneurship.

So, entertaining at least the possibility that we have access to this power, how do we shift our mindset that chains us to the world around us, to one that sets us free? The answer to which must also have the potential to liberate the entrepreneur from their struggle.

Firstly, we need to explore the realms of being that are available to us…

Consciousness

Most of us are familiar with three states of what we call consciousness: being awake, being asleep with dreaming, and deep sleep with no dreaming. The latter is 'unconscious' and we take it in good faith that it exists when we are neither awake nor dreaming.

We loosely classify these different experiences of being as states of consciousness - the degree to which we are aware of ourselves and the world around us. The Vedic tradition of ancient India has studied and codified these states, identifying four:

Jagruti is the waking state. There are degrees of being awake which mean that I cannot attempt a crossword puzzle before reaching a certain level of wakefulness. Some of us even need coffee to get there!

Svapna is the dream state. Dreams can be much more vivid than everyday life. For this reason, this state is considered more psychologically profound than our waking state, even though it is physically inert. Remember that thought is more real than matter.

Sushupti is dreamless sleep but with awareness. This is beyond the average human experience and can be explored in a yogic method called Yoga Nidra.

Finally, Turya is pure consciousness unsullied by memory and therefore beyond time, fully present with no past or future. This 'state' can be experienced momentarily at the point of waking from sleep. Sometimes dramatic or traumatic events can invoke it.

In the English language we conflate wakefulness and consciousness. In reality, the two are quite distinct.

Many teachings, ancient and modern, assert that consciousness is not personalised, it exists in all matter and pervades all space. So it's important to grasp that we may not be generating different degrees of consciousness - even though that is how we experience it - but accessing different levels - rather like an electron might shift its orbit from a lower to a higher one. The orbits exist independently of the electrons.

Thus, how awake you may feel is not necessarily related to the level of consciousness you have access to.

The waking state is likely the one you are most familiar with.

It is the one in which we 'get things done' and is generally considered to be the only one of value in our activity-focused society.

The Indian mystic Sadhguru likens consciousness to the air within a soap bubble. Although there is a barrier of soap between my bubble and yours, the contents are identical. When the bubbles burst there is no difference between the two. We are each a piece of consciousness.

The implications of this are profound - contrary to what our senses, our mind, our thinking and feeling tell us, we are neither our bodies, our minds, our thoughts nor our feelings. We are simply consciousness. This is what we are - everything else has been accrued and is what we have.

You cannot be what you have, only what you are.

FEELINGS

How we feel is the dominant factor in our experience of life. We do things to feel better. Even an altruistic act of charity has a feel-good payback. No one in their right minds would do anything to feel worse - even 'cutting one's nose off to spite one's face', metaphorically speaking, will return some warped sense of satisfaction. All action is intended to make us feel better. There are no exceptions.

The neuroscientist, Antonio Damasio, has demonstrated beyond reasonable doubt that all our decisions are based on feeling, never reason. Impairment of feeling impedes decision-making to the point of: no feeling - no decision. Fortunately, in functional minds at least, reason, logic, rationale and analysis serve to inform the way we feel before we go on to make decisions.

Have you noticed a propensity to go with a decision that feels absolutely right (to the point of being choiceless) and then retrospectively justify it with some plausible reasoning?

So the way we feel is central to our experience of life and the actions we take. These feelings take on a variety of tone and intensity, well-documented by psychologists, from the ecstatic to the suicidal, from serenity to outrage.

In 1980, Robert Plutchik proposed a wheel of emotions depicting eight primary, bipolar emotions from which other emotions are derived - not dissimilar from the mixing of primary colours to generate a full spectrum. Today other theories suggest anything from four to 27 emotions which, if nothing else, provides evidence that emotions are not rational!

But what about the difference between feelings and emotions - two words that most of us use synonymously?

A useful distinction I find is to consider emotions as the transient reactions to thinking and perception. An event, a thought, a memory can all trigger a consequent emotion. A single day can be filled with scores of emotional highs and lows according to the thoughts we think, whether they originate in perception, memory or imagination. Feelings, on the other hand, constitute our emotional foundation or baseline, which is less susceptible to circumstance and the passing of time. On this basis we can depict the relationship between thought, emotion and feeling thus:

$$\text{Thought} \rightarrow \text{Emotion} \rightarrow \text{Feeling}$$

At this point it is imperative to recognise that emotions arriving through perception of events are not caused by the events themselves, but by our thinking, triggered by the event. Which explains how the same event can affect different people in very different ways.

In other words, there is no essential difference in the quality of emotion generated by a thought, a memory, an imagining or an event.

The reason this is so important is that it allows us to disconnect the way we feel from the circumstances we find ourselves in. Realising that it is our thinking that leads to the way we feel, via emotion, gives us the option to intervene in the apparent chain of cause and effect, and decide to regulate our thinking in order to change the way we feel. However, this only becomes a possibility when we choose to exercise discretion over the thoughts that we think, whilst recognising that they are more real than the events we witness through our senses.

Taking the entrepreneurial leap and beginning any significant undertaking immediately exposes the entrepreneur to events, situations and imagined possibilities far beyond the comfort of normality. Uncertainty, risk, complexity and doubt provide fertile ground for a helter-skelter of emotions that can easily overwhelm those of us not disciplined in the regulation of these inner dynamics.

But regulation does not mean thought-control…

THINKING

Back in the 17th century, Rene Descartes revived a version of mind-body dualism, stating that the mental can exist outside of the body, and the body cannot think. Today we have sound evidence that at least some thought, if not all, takes place in the brain - an organ firmly rooted in the physical body. Eastern philosophy takes this one step further stating that the brain is no more than another organ within the human body, akin to the liver, heart, guts etc. and that intelligence is distributed.

The brain's function is to think, just as the heart's is to pump and the kidneys' is to cleanse blood. Although there is some evidence to suggest that, with training, you can influence your heart rate consciously, a healthy heart is generally best left to its own devices - it knows what to do in the best interests of the body. Similarly, the idea of consciously intervening in your liver function sounds quite absurd in the knowledge that the liver is better equipped than we are to do its job.

What if, the brain being just another organ, is also best left to get on with what it does best which, amongst other things that we are not conscious of, is to think? What if, attempting to intervene in this natural process is counterproductive?

To get a sense of this rather counterintuitive suggestion, try the following experiment right now:

Stop Thinking

Empty your mind and stop all thought dead.

How did that go for you? Were you successful?

If you found that a challenge or weren't quite sure if you succeeded or not, try this instead:

Do not think about a flying hippopotamus

Spend the next minute avoiding any thought about airborne hippos.

Chances are that you were not fully successful at either task. There is good reason that we are better off failing at both:

Firstly, you need to maintain the thinking function for survival purposes. It would be somewhat perilous to turn off thinking and consequently forfeit the ability to switch it back on again. You need thinking to fulfil the most basic requirements of human life.

Secondly, your brain knows what thought to think better than you do and, fortunately, it's not going to take much notice of your attempt to interfere by telling it what it can't think about. The stream of thoughts that the brain will offer you is the basis of creativity, choice and abundance. This is what it is meant to do.

That may well sound like bad news if you suffer from an over-active mind - one that seems to flood you with unwanted thoughts and attendant emotions, draining your energy and offering no respite from the anxiety that often accompanies it.

But in practice it's very good news - your brain is doing exactly what it should be doing. The dysfunction is occurring further up the cognitive hierarchy.

A few years ago I used to enjoy watching both my sons play rugby on a Saturday morning. Because of their age difference, they very rarely played together, so I would happily watch two matches in succession. On a few occasions, their matches would be scheduled to play concurrently, usually on adjacent pitches, whereupon I would stand strategically between the fields so that I could watch both matches simultaneously. A perfect solution, or so I thought. My actual experience was of not really watching either match as I continually flitted my attention between them.

Imagine having an array of 10 large TVs in your living room, each connected to a different channel, each showing a different, favourite drama, sport, film, news programme etc. Technically, eminently possible - practically, a complete waste of time. Even the most fervent addict of Netflix shows wouldn't bother trying to watch more than one series simultaneously. But if you did attempt to watch more than one channel at a time, only to discover its futility, would you blame the technology, or would you recognise that your choice to watch multiple streams of information in parallel was at fault?

Absurd as this may appear, this is exactly what we do with our thinking apparatus, habitually and unconsciously. The phenomenon of scattered attention is well known and documented in ancient and modern esoteric traditions. Even today there is a growing awareness of the inefficiency of 'multitasking' as we skim from Facebook to WhatsApp to Google to YouTube and back again.

Our brains will provide all the thinking we can deal with, and plenty more. Regulation is essential, but not at the level of thought. It has to be at the higher level of attention. Attention - our ability to be aware of something - is the only thing we have full control over - since every word we utter and every action we take starts with paying attention to a thought.

The quality of that attention determines the quality of our speech, the actions we take, the relationships we form, the responsibilities we undertake and ultimately, the life we live. Considered from this perspective, the quality and direction of our attention is the only variable we have total control over - and it is the only one we need control of.

When you real-ise (make real) this perspective, some very profound and intriguing things start to happen:

It begins to dawn that who you think you are is an artefact that is really not you at all. You realise that you are not the thoughts and feelings that you experience, but rather the experiencer itself.

The belief systems that you identify with - which are no more than complexes of ideas that you are invested in - begin to lose their attraction. You start to hold them more loosely, seeing that they too are just ideas and that their allure comes from the life you give them.

Emotions become less volatile as the thoughts behind them garner less of your energy. Understanding your relationship to thinking and feeling affords you discretion over the quality and intensity of your emotions.

Your feeling foundation - the baseline of how you feel from day to day - rises to encompass more joy, happiness, love, fulfilment and value. It becomes less perturbed by the events and circumstances you find yourself in.

You begin to catch glimpses of how, in this state of consciousness, it isn't the world around you that is responsible for how you feel, but the complete reverse: the world around you reflects back your feelings like a giant mirror.

Liberated from the tyranny of thought and the illusion that we are what we think and feel, we become free to create the feeling world that we want to live in. This then becomes a life-changing super-power.

We can pay attention to just one of the 10 screens in front of us and absorb a coherent and complete stream of information. We can watch a single rugby match. We can write one word at a time in completing our latest best-seller.

So the regulation we seek is not exercised at the level of thinking, which is just an autonomic human function. It is found higher up the chain of command in the ability to direct and focus our attention, and to maintain it. Managing attention will afford us the ability to determine what kind of thoughts and emotions we entertain and, as a consequence, how we feel.

Being able to take responsibility for, and managing how we feel, gives us enormous power and potential. The better we feel:

- the better we can respond to circumstance
- the stronger our relationships become
- the clearer our thinking becomes
- the more integrated we feel
- the more healthy we feel, physically and mentally
- the brighter our futures appear
- the more imaginative and creative we can be

But - and this is a big but - these benefits only manifest once we are prepared to abandon the belief that how we feel is wholly dependent on what we experience. After decades of practising and identifying with this assumption, we're adept at it and it may not suddenly evaporate. Yet neither is it confined to a linear progression - it is within our gift, now.

MINDSETS

According to Wikipedia, a mindset is an "established set of attitudes, esp. regarded as typical of a particular group's social or cultural values; the outlook, philosophy, or values of a person; (now also more generally) frame of mind, attitude, and disposition."

Definitions of mindset vary, but tend to incorporate other psychological concepts such as opinions, beliefs, perspective, etc. I shall use the word to denote a complex of beliefs which changes the way we perceive the world around us - a belief being an idea that we are invested in to some degree and are prepared to defend as right, true, or good. To date, I have not met one person who would sincerely defend an idea that they feel is wrong or bad.

In 2006, Carol Dweck published Mindset: The New Psychology of Success, in which she described fixed and growth mindsets. Those with a fixed mindset believe intelligence, talent, and other qualities are innate and unchangeable. A growth mindset means that people believe their intelligence and talents can be improved through effort and application. They may be unaware of their mindsets but the impact of a fixed or growth mindset will be there for all to see.

The difference between these two mindsets becomes starkly apparent when the individual encounters a failure. Those with a growth mindset will learn and re-apply themselves to find solutions. Those with a fixed mindset will determine that the problem is insurmountable and give up.

Clearly, in a world fixated with successful outcomes, growth mindsets are deemed good and fixed ones are not. My contention, in contrast, is that all mindsets impose limitations upon us, whether they are of the growth or fixed variety.

The clue is in the name. We know from objective science that our minds are neuroplastic - denoting the brain's ability to form new neural connections throughout our life. We know subjectively that our beliefs and perspectives change with experience. A healthy mind cannot be set - it has to be open to change - accepting impressions that impact the neural network. A truly set mind is pathologically abnormal - not a mind at all.

By this token, all mindsets are capable of restricting us if the degree to which we are identified with them prevents us from seeing them for what they are.

In fact, I would suggest that the degree of investment in a mindset is of far more significance than the mindset itself. The more we identify with an idea, the less able we are to respond intelligently to real circumstances.

A few years back, a managing director asked me, as a non-executive director, to attend the dismissal of a senior manager who was falling far short of performance targets. The MD is a caring, thoughtful type who believes himself to be a considerate and compassionate leader.

After some prevarication, the MD eventually got to the point, informing the sales manager that his contract was being terminated. At this point, his mindset took control and he spent the next 10 minutes apologising for the decision, telling the sales manager how sympathetic he was to his plight. The 'compassion' intensified with the MD close to tears, feeling distraught on behalf of his ex-employee. He was, in his own way, demonstrating how much he cared for his people.

Meanwhile, the sales manager was becoming visibly more agitated. Frustration was turning to anger as he endured a mawkish display of unwanted sentiment which was evidently more about assuaging the MD's guilt than any true compassion.

Had the MD had the self-awareness to give the sales manager what he really needed - a brief, courteous thank you and goodbye - everyone's emotions would have been saved a great deal of turmoil. Instead, the MD indulged his tightly held belief-system - his mindset - desperately trying to present himself as a caring, sympathetic boss, regardless of what the situation required.

In our everyday state of consciousness, growth mindsets are undoubtedly more desirable than fixed mindsets. But even a growth mindset that is held tightly will imprison, not liberate.

In early 2023, two national leaders made global headlines with news of early resignations. Jacinda Ardern, New Zealand's prime minister admitted that she "no longer had enough in the tank" to continue in post. Less than a month later, Nicola Sturgeon, the first minister of Scotland, followed suit citing insufficient energy to fulfil her term. Many commentators have described both leaders as victims of burnout.

Both their supporters and detractors seemed to agree that their premature resignations set back their respective political causes and compromised many of the advances they were associated with. From a party political perspective, their actions were unequivocally counter-productive, at least in the short-term.

No one could accuse these ultra-high achievers of having anything other than a growth mindset - for themselves, their parties and the countries they led. Yet it is the same growth mindset that eventually compromised their wellbeing and brought their careers to a sudden and unexpected halt.

In politicians, mindsets often manifest as ideologies - a set of a priori beliefs which the individual holds as self-evident and incontrovertible. The degree with which these ideas are held as absolute - the depth of identification with them - often reflects in the separation from their polar opposites. Hard left and hard right are unlikely to ever reconcile. Furthermore, many of humanity's biggest mistakes are associated with absolutist ideologies that could not be questioned without fear of reprisal.

Again, it is not so much the specifics of the ideas that are problematic, as the fervour with which they are idolised and then defended.

The following Daoist parable elegantly illustrates how it is possible to transcend mindset and the reactions they impose on us, through non-judgement, and non-attachment to those ideas that many of us take as given:

A long time ago, a poor Chinese farmer lost a horse. All the neighbours came around and said, "Well that's too bad." The farmer said, "Maybe."

Shortly after, the horse returned bringing another horse with him. All the neighbours came around again and said, "Well that's good fortune," to which the farmer replied, "Maybe."

The next day, the farmer's son was trying to tame the new horse and fell, breaking his leg. All the neighbours came around and said, "Well that's too bad," and the farmer replied, "Maybe."

The following day soldiers came and took away all the able-bodied young men to fight in the army. Many were killed or injured but the farmer's son was left behind. "You are so lucky!" his neighbours cried. "Maybe," the farmer replied.

So how do we weaken our attachment to conscious and subconscious mindsets? The first step is to be aware of them, but without intervention - just observation. Here are some tactics to practise:

The next time you hear views that are at odds with yours, be aware of the feelings that the variance creates. Just watch.

Resist the urge to react.

Remember that the feeling that you are right and the other is wrong is identical in the other. Only the thinking is different.

Wanting to dismiss opposing views is a symptom of extremism and zealotry - remember the mindset is not the person, however identified they are.

Identify the views you share in common - inevitably they will outnumber those you don't.

Mindsets appear in forms other than rationalised ideologies. They also manifest as bias, prejudice, intolerance and bigotry. A similar mechanism lumps particular group characteristics or stereotypes together to create difference and separation. The choice is broad: class, gender, ethnicity, language, accent, colour, height, weight, religion, profession etc. etc.

I would suggest that none of us are free from this form of dualism, simply because the process of categorisation and differentiation is established as a habit of mind - and very useful in the right context. But when it is used to sever the relationships between fellow human beings and separate us, it undermines our wellbeing and threatens our humanity.

It is enticing to address the impact of others' mindsets, and is undoubtedly right, in some instances, to legislate against them. Yet the focus is inevitably on everyone else - rarely oneself. Matthew's biblical question holds good here:

And why beholdest thou the mote that is in thy brother's eye, but considerest not the beam that is in thine own eye?

The world we experience provides us with an excellent mirror, reflecting back at us - often through the behaviour of others - exactly what we need to perceive in ourselves. The intensity of our own reaction to others' mindsets is perhaps indicative of the strength of our own.

Maybe the most pernicious mindset of them all is the belief that I am aware of my mindset and yours, but you are blissfully ignorant of both.

Takeaways

- Imagination is more real than 'reality'
- Consciousness is not personal
- You don't think - thinking happens
- Your attention is the only thing to regulate
- Mindsets are good and bad but all limit perception
- Look to your own mindsets before those of others
- The world reflects back what you pay attention to

LESS PUSH, MORE FLOW

The right mixture of custard powder and water (no sugar required) creates a non-newtonian fluid that has an interesting property. You can stir it and pour it as a slightly less fluid version of water. But, you can also run across its surface without sinking into it. The viscosity of the liquid changes with the pressure you apply to it.

I first discovered this as a helpful child, making custard for the family - or rather myself. Stirring the mixture of milk and powder (which is mainly cornflour) I noticed that as I speeded up, beyond a certain point the liquid would suddenly stiffen and provide much more resistance to the stirring.

It was almost as if the mixture was telling me that I really didn't need to be so vigorous - gentle stirring was enough and anything more would be resisted. So I had a choice, be moderate and allow the liquid to flow easily, or push hard and struggle to stir it at all.

Search for 'non-newtonian fluid' on YouTube and you will find entertaining videos demonstrating how you can easily dip a pencil into a cornflour-water mixture, but if you hit it hard with a hammer, you cannot break the surface.

This behaviour makes an elegant analogy for business - particularly entrepreneurial business which is frequently set on making the maximum impact in the minimum time. Stirring the custard as quickly as possible, you might say - even hitting it with a hammer.

Have you ever been in a situation in which you are taking action and expecting a timely result? You have put all your resources and energy into setting things up to mitigate any resistance and promote a favourable and prompt outcome. A house purchase, a sales campaign, a recruitment drive - whatever it may be. And yet the result is elusive; things drag, people procrastinate, obstacles arise. Or maybe nothing visible is responsible for the delay, yet it persists. Sometimes the blockage clears, sometimes it takes way longer than anyone predicted. Occasionally the project simply aborts and never reaches fruition.

This is not just a common occurrence, it is endemic in the human experience and part of the uncertainty in which we seem to be immersed. The question is not so much how to avoid these dynamics, as how to navigate them.

You may also have noticed how pushing for the result you want, when you want it, frequently meets with the kind of resistance that custard mix provides when you try to stir it too vigorously. You can expend the extra energy to no benefit at all. If you enjoy the exertion, all well and good, but most of us don't - we are only prepared to invest time, energy, attention and resources to expedite and guarantee the desired outcome. Which means that when we do, and our efforts are thwarted, there is an emotional backlash of irritation, frustration, criticism, anger - even fear and shame.

At a corporate level, the pressure to release products before they are ready can be so intense as to be irresistible. In 2006, Microsoft launched Vista. The software had so many compatibility and performance problems that even Microsoft's most loyal customers turned against it. Even with a $500 million marketing budget, the operating system flopped badly enough for Apple to lampoon it in an advertising campaign. The need for further development and bug-fixing was sacrificed for a timely launch and justified by the theoretical ease with which software can be upgraded. In other words, process was surrendered to outcome, in marked contrast to the approach of Edison, Wiles and many other successful entrepreneurs.

We often perceive the combination of the situation and our reaction to it as one and the same, naming it struggle. But in reality, they are quite separate, just as the custard mix is not the mixer. The object of our efforts is simply obeying laws, whether or not they are known to us. So our reaction cannot be an upshot of what is, or is not taking place - it can only be a result of the expectations we have chosen to impose. The struggle is purely and uniquely of our own making.

An Antidote To Struggle

How do high-achieving, smart, energetic, capable entrepreneurs get into these states of mind?

The answer is simply down to the levels of consciousness that we inhabit. It's not down to how awake we are or how alert we are - no one is asleep on the job. It's not down to lack of intellect or the capacity to get things done.

It is a function of how aligned you are with the truth of who you are.

What on earth does that mean? It means that the more you identify with ideas about who and what you are, the more distant you are from the truth. Ideas and thoughts about who we are can never be the reality, only pale shadows of it. Ideas are accrued and, to repeat, we cannot be what we have, only what we are.

Take the sentence: "I am a successful entrepreneur". A successful entrepreneur is an idea that you (and others) hold about you - it is relative and subject to change. You may feel successful today, and an abject failure tomorrow. But it is only the I am that is aware of this. The I am is the conscious observer or witness that observes no matter what. It is beyond any condition such as being successful. It is just consciousness and never subject to qualification.

This is not some lofty metaphysical principle - it is available as direct experience to all of us, at every moment, providing we are willing to forsake analysis and judgement in favour of experiential perception. In other terms, thinking about consciousness is like reading a map instead of taking a walk. Thought is not the reality, just as the map is not the territory.

The degree to which we are conscious of the relationship between who we are and who we think we are, equates to the level of consciousness that we live in. Just like the electron mentioned previously, we have the option of raising or lowering our consciousness. The more conscious we are, the more aligned we are with the truth of who we are. This truth is beyond intellect, identity and beliefs and beyond time - it simply is. It is also beyond explanation and description, yet it is our essence. It needs no esoteric, religious or spiritual context.

From this conscious perspective, we know (beyond belief) that any struggle is a self-constructed artifice, seemingly designed to lure us into the false belief that we are failing and that we should suffer as a consequence. Exactly how you fail and suffer is down to your identity, experiences and beliefs. Which is why we all do it differently, if at all.

The antidote to struggle is simply a higher level of consciousness in which the struggle doesn't so much diminish, as ceases to exist. Just as the idea of a flat earth cannot persist when you view our planet from space, so false ideas cannot survive conscious observation - rather like vampires, they have to avoid the light to stay alive and continue feeding off their host.

So, how do we facilitate this conscious shift, taking quantum leaps from one level of consciousness to another?

Paradoxically, the best starting point is one of unknowing. If we are looking to disentangle ourselves from false ideas of identity - and if any idea is only a representation of who we are, never the reality - then we need to be wary of taking on any new identities, however attractive they may be.

The Yogic mantra neti neti is Sanskrit for *not this, not this*. It is used to remind the meditator that whatever they think, that is not reality. For busy entrepreneurs, it is enough to begin to remind yourself that your beliefs and mindsets - particularly those you hold about yourself - will be getting in the way of realising who you really are, holding you in lower levels of consciousness. Annihilating these ideas is not the objective - remember we cannot directly control our discursive minds. Seeing the ideas clearly for what they are is the first step that inevitably loosens the grip we hold on them. Holding ideas - any idea - loosely so they can be let go, is the objective.

THE MONKEY GRIP

Years ago my 12 year old son referred to his father's "sad little job" at a dinner party with adult friends and colleagues. My immediate inner reaction was one of anger - rage in fact. How dare a mere child show contempt and disrespect for my efforts to provide for him and the family? I felt the anger grow, but I also clearly saw the identity from which it sprang -

a self-important, somewhat conceited and insecure figure that was, at the time, experiencing frustration from apparent lack of success. I was struggling and I didn't want the world to know, so I had constructed a persona to compensate for it. The complex of beliefs behind the persona - my identity - had been attacked and I was going to fight back.

As this construct came into focus, I realised what it was and my relationship to it. I was reminded that I was not this. Immediately the anger evaporated and I was able to laugh sincerely along with everyone else at the table. It was a huge relief that I no longer had to expend energy in order to maintain and defend these false beliefs about myself. But it didn't stop there. Not only did the overly inflated ideas of self-esteem disappear, so did the self-inflicted judgements of failure. I was free from both and felt entirely liberated as a result. The struggle dematerialised.

•

Water can be a scarce commodity in Africa and finding it can be greatly simplified by using the services of a baboon. The trick is to feed the monkey salt, wait for it to get thirsty and then follow it to a source of water. To prevent the monkey from going elsewhere before it gets thirsty, it must be caught harmlessly first. This is done by digging a small hole in a termite hill and inserting some melon seeds, in full view of the baboon.

The baboon's curiosity gets the better of him and eventually he goes over to the mound and puts his hand in the hole. He finds the seeds and grabs them, but the size of his fist makes it impossible to withdraw without first releasing the seeds. The monkey will not let go and creates a huge drama over his predicament. Even though he could escape at any moment, he chooses to struggle instead. In the meantime, his trapper can slip a rope over his neck and detain him. Finally he submits and relinquishes his prize. The monkey now feasts on the salt and the next morning is so parched that he will go straight to his source of water, revealing its whereabouts to any follower.

Make no mistake - we are that monkey, grasping on to what we hold precious, like grim death. We refuse to let go, even though releasing our 'treasure' would set us free. We would rather be subservient to external forces than risk losing our heart's desire.

Tolkien's The Lord of the Rings offers a similar parable of the thrall in which we can be held by those things we covet. But Gollum's treasure - his 'precious' - is a metaphor for a far more bewitching and powerful possession than a mere ring, whatever its attraction. These are the stories we tell ourselves, the identities, the egos and the belief-systems that we hold dear. They do not simply attract us, they are us - and any threat of separation provokes an immediate existential crisis.

Ultimately, letting go is the only practical strategy and whether or not the release is chosen or enforced by circumstance, the outcome, sooner or later, is a shift in consciousness reflecting the knowledge that we are not what we thought we were.

In our attempts to raise the orbit of consciousness that we inhabit, our most powerful tool is consciousness itself. In practical terms, this means awareness of and attention to, not just what is going on in the world around us, which entrepreneurs tend to be well-versed in, but what is going on within us. This is where the real action is and where the levers of change lie. It is also the true target of that very topical subject: mindfulness.

As one develops the ability to hold ideas and beliefs less tightly, the nature of struggle changes markedly. Firstly, the actions you take become less reactive and more responsive. Reactive behaviour always originates in the past, from established patterns of thinking, feeling and behaviour - habits - practised over the years. It is essentially unconscious behaviour which excludes free will. Responsive behaviour is fully conscious and allows intelligence and free will to be brought to bear in the moment - unfettered by past events.

Secondly, the emotional fallout of events is greatly reduced and the ability to restore equilibrium - resilience - is increased and accelerated.

But perhaps the greatest benefit, and the focus of this chapter, is the realisation that the pushing, shoving and struggling to achieve your goals - like the strenuous stirring of custard mix - is a waste of time and energy that will not only fail to manifest the desired outcome, but actively keep it at bay.

Any enterprise, just like making custard, will flow smoothly at a rate beyond which invites struggle. Unfortunately for those of us wanting to cling to some semblance of predictability, the rate at which an enterprise will flow is a function of many variables, including time itself. The upside of this uncertainty is that it invites the entrepreneur to 'feel into' the flow, avoiding struggle in the process.

The big mistake that so many of us make is to expect the flow to be faster than it wants to be. This is a major contributory factor to struggle, overwhelm, clinical anxiety, burnout, depression, failure and worse. The tragedy is that all of these debilitating symptoms are screaming at the entrepreneur to stop, just for a moment, and find a different way that respects the realities of entrepreneurial activity.

Mindfulness is the shortcut to accessing higher states of consciousness. It is brought about by focusing attention on the present - the now moment. The habitual state of consciousness for many of us is a mix of random perceptions of the world around us - courtesy of our five senses - and a stream of thoughts emanating from memory and imagination, conditioned by intellect and identity. This is a state of scattered attention in which little of note takes place. Sooner or later, life compels us to take constructive action which requires a higher degree of focus. We explore this further in a subsequent chapter.

PUSHING FOR GROWTH

Growth is a good example of a desirable process that is best not hurried. We all know instinctively that good growth is natural and organic, best left well alone in many circumstances. No gardener in their right mind would dig up a seed to check on its progress.

The thought of artificially accelerating the physical growth of a child, for instance, is abhorrent to most of us. Many countries ban the use of hormones in animal feeds, whilst the increased availability of organic grain, fruit and vegetables - free from synthetic fertilisers, has been notable.

Yet the demand for growth is insatiable. There seems to be a universal law of expansion that compels growth. And when the individual life-form becomes unable to grow further, it sacrifices itself for the growth of others. As the universe expands macrocosmically, so does plant, animal and human life, at a microcosmic scale.

The law of expansion is mirrored in the human realm, which aspires to be bigger, faster and better at all levels of activity. Markets fuel the growth by rewarding it and incentivising more output for proportionately less input. The urge for growth is inexorable and perhaps nowhere more evident than in the heart of the entrepreneur.

Be under no illusion - growth is good. Life is expansion, experience, novelty, innovation, creativity, imagination - growth.

But growth is a function of time and subject to its laws. We can accelerate growth, but only for a Faustian payback. Promoting crop yield through fertilisation has long-term implications for the soil, ultimately rendering it infertile. The EU has banned the use of hormones in cattle to boost their growth due to neurological, developmental and carcinogenic risks.

The many schemes designed to speed entrepreneurial growth by lowering the barrier to entry may well have created more enterprises, but only whilst also attracting the 50% doomed to failure within 5 years.

Those entrepreneurs skilful enough to attract private equity in order to accelerate their business growth, often find themselves compelled to supercharge every aspect of the venture. Many end up on the insatiable hamster-wheel of RoI - return on investment. The business benefits don't always compensate for the personal sacrifices, with many entrepreneurs paying not just with sweat but with their health, relationships and equanimity. For some, it presents as a zero-sum game.

Of the most frequent unfulfilled aspirations that the elderly lament as they approach the final chapters of their lives, "I wish I'd worked harder" is not on the list. The opposite statement lies near the top.

Scaled up, we find institutional shareholders baying for returns and share-price growth on a quarterly basis. CEOs are hired or fired for their ability to satisfy the instant gratification of the markets, frequently paying a price for both failure and 'success'.

Warren Buffet, one of the most successful investors of all time takes a much longer term view: "If you aren't willing to own a stock for ten years, don't even think about owning it for ten minutes." The wisdom behind this contrarian view is twofold: firstly, the realisation that share value and operational value are quite distinct variables; secondly, over time, the share price will be compelled, behind any volatility, to follow the operational reality. Only with time will the share price begin to accurately reflect the real value of the business. The process will not be hurried.

Stirring the custard beyond the point at which it begins to push back will have some impact - perhaps not least the impression that one is working hard. The busy fool is happy as long as he is doing something… anything.

Who, other than a fool, would want to hurry life - the ultimate expression of growth - in order to accelerate the arrival of its ultimate conclusion?

In the next couple of chapters, we'll be looking at what needs to be in place to support the flow and make any need to push or struggle entirely redundant.

Takeaways

- Processes have a natural tempo beyond which they push back

- The antidote to struggle is consciousness - the truth of who you are

- Holding on to stories about ourselves creates the struggle

- Letting go of who we think we are is the ultimate liberation

- Accelerating growth beyond its natural tempo creates imbalance

- Respecting the natural pace of growth makes it more successful and pleasant

THE INNER FLOW OF PURPOSE

Deep within every human being lies a sense of purpose and the urge to express it through our lives on planet Earth. For some, purpose burns bright and clear and drives the individual to extraordinary experiences and accomplishments. For others it has become obscured and diminished over time to the point where life seems mundane and mediocre, sometimes even intolerable.

The word purpose, literally means: that which you put forth. It has a sense of flow or expression - a pressing out or a projection.

As children, the urge to express naturally manifests in us as play - curiosity drives exploration all within an ambience of joy and fun. The child will build a castle, draw a picture, fight imaginary dragons - each creation being quickly and easily abandoned for a new possibility. Their attention is seemingly on the fun of creation, not so much on what is created.

If you were to ask them what their purpose is - or as Simon Sinek asks: what is your why? - they might well look at you quizzically for a moment, and carry on playing.

Let us now ask a similar question of those that have had extraordinary impact over the course of their lives. What was the common purpose of the likes of Socrates, Jesus, Buddha, Leonardo, Newton, Shakespeare, Martin Luther King, Henry Ford - all of whom invested their energies in very different pursuits and to different ends?

Finally, what is the common purpose behind all activity, whether that of a child, a genius, or you and me?

I would suggest that our primary purpose in life is to create - that is, to bring into being. The original meaning of the Latin root creare was to make grow, thus expanding the meaning to include the development of things already in existence. So the common factor in all human activity is to bring into being and develop whatever you choose: ideas, insights, technology, art, experiences, relationships, society - the list is endless.

None of us can live a life without creation. For an entrepreneur, it is the raison d'être. It is the process of creating that keeps us alive and provides the meaning, fulfilment and freedom we crave. The urge to create needs to express itself - it needs to flow.

So great is this drive that the act of creation seems to take precedence over whatever is created. The process eclipses the result. Children seem to know this intuitively, flitting from one creation to another without much attachment to whatever they create. Adults have more difficulty in maintaining this flow, tending to fixate more on the output than the activity, with the possible exception of procreation!

The balance of focus between process and result is critically important. When it is skewed in favour of the outcome, the end starts to justify the means and strange things happen.

We can witness this in sport, when the urge to win can compel the competitors to move beyond the spirit of the game, eventually compromising their integrity through cheating, bad sportsmanship and even violence. Any enjoyment is forfeited. This delicate balance is elegantly described by Grantland Rice in one of his many sporting insights:

> When the One Great Scorer
> comes to write against your name,
> He marks, not that you won or lost,
> but how you played the game.

Yet, without a powerful urge to overcome your adversary - to win - the sport provides little appeal or spectacle.

I would frequently discuss this with my sons, both of whom have played contact sports internationally. Despite their protestations that winning was the sole objective, at almost any cost, they clearly derived great satisfaction from playing, enthusiastically taking part even when losing seemed almost inevitable.

On the subject of losing, I recall, somewhat foolishly,

declaring to a group of alpha-male school dads that losing at sport was more valuable than winning, as losing taught you to deal with a mix of negative emotions in a positive way. They, in contrast, were under no illusion that the purpose of sport was to win, that losing was failure, and that I was a loser!

The inconvenient fact is that however successful you are as a sportsperson, you will lose sooner or later. So, as Rudyard Kipling famously declared:

> If you can meet with Triumph and Disaster
> And treat those two impostors just the same…
> …you'll be a Man, my son!

As some Olympic athletes experience, if the final result is all that matters, even a gold medal can leave you a victim of 'summit syndrome', with a sudden loss of 'purpose' and nothing more to aim for. Mental health is a recognised challenge in the world of elite sport - one study of 50 swimmers competing for positions in Canada's Olympic and world championship teams, found that before competition, 68% of them "met the criteria for a major depressive episode".

The following story illustrates how the focus of activity can radically change outcomes:

Two pottery classes were asked to complete different projects. One was asked to create the best pot they could. The second was asked to create as many pots as possible. The first class set about researching what the best pot looked like and how to create it. The second class just threw themselves into the task, churning out pot after pot. After a couple of weeks, the classes were asked to enter their best pot into a competition. Not only did the class that was asked to create many pots win the competition, many of their pots were judged to be better than the few pots the other class had produced in their quest for the best pot. In other words the focus on creation was more successful than the pursuit of excellence.

Oak trees (and many other species) mirror this behaviour by producing up to 90,000 acorns in a season, many times more than will ever develop into new oaks. The entrepreneur Thomas Edison required several thousand iterations of his light bulb before he hit upon one that could be commercialised.

A conclusion that is difficult to avoid drawing from these examples is that expression of purpose creates more value than striving for a particular result. But why?

A simple, practical reason is that we can never guarantee a particular future outcome, but we can always decide what we do right now.

A metaphysical reason is that expression of purpose brings you into the present moment, where all our power resides. Whereas prioritising the future can only dilute, undermine even, our connection to now and consequently our state of consciousness and the power that goes with it.

Purpose, then, is less to do with the fruits of your labours, more to do with the labours themselves. And this mirrors life itself, which for me, and hopefully for you too, is more about the experience of living than obsessing over its finale.

The inference to take with us as entrepreneurs is that our purpose needs to be an expression of how we dedicate our time and energies in the moment, rather than any particular outcome we are seeking to manifest.

My own purpose is not to write a book, which can only be the culmination of months of work and decades of experience, but to clarify the business of leadership and entrepreneurship - for myself and others - from hour to hour and day to day.

One reason that entrepreneurs frequently struggle is that they mistake their purpose for their goal. In the following chapter we'll be exploring goals in terms of vision - a critical element in the entrepreneur's life but quite distinct from purpose. Vision is a product of the imagination, yet to manifest. Purpose can only be expressed in the here and now.

To successfully express your purpose as an entrepreneur, two inner qualities are required to support the flow that we seek.

INTEGRITY

The first of these is Integrity. Integrity is a much misunderstood entrepreneurial trait, generally believed to derive from honesty and living according to moral principle.

The counterintuitive reality is that both honesty and principle detract from true integrity. How is that possible when we are told at every turn that people with integrity are truthful and principled?

Principles, by definition, are absolutes that apply in all circumstances. A simple example is Archimedes' Principle, which states that: the upward buoyant force exerted on a body immersed in a fluid, is equal to the weight of the fluid displaced. This principle holds good whether you're on Earth, the Moon or even in outer space. A possible exception could be within a black hole but this is not a circumstance anyone will experience anytime soon.

Absolute honesty, in contrast, will fail to benefit anyone in many everyday scenarios. Lying by omission - the act of withholding truth, opinion or observation - is a basic survival tactic that we employ daily to maintain functional relationships with those around us. Just imagine sharing every impression, thought and judgement about another with no filter in place.

Few of us would not lie directly to protect others or ourselves from harm and be very clear that it was the right course of action. So honesty cannot be a moral imperative, less still an inviolable principle. Similarly, other principles are quite easy to expose as conditional, never absolute. Being nice to people is a wonderful thing indeed, but being nice to everyone at all times and at any cost may not be for the greater good.

The same cannot be said of integrity which needs to hold good in all circumstances. Is there any situation in which compromising your integrity would benefit anyone at all - you included? On that basis, integrity cannot embrace principles that are conditional on circumstance and open to interpretation.

So what is integrity? Quite simply, it means whole, complete or sound. A building has integrity when it has all three of those qualities and stands on its own. Similarly, we humans have integrity when we are complete within ourselves, knowing and feeling that wholeness.

If a building requires scaffolding or any external support to keep it safe and upright, we can conclude that it is not complete in itself and therefore lacks structural integrity. So too we can say that any human reliant on external frames of reference - principles, morals, ethics, rules, regulations - to function effectively, lacks integrity.

Now, I am not claiming for a moment that moral or ethical behaviour demonstrates lack of integrity. I am suggesting that there is a lack of integrity when one's behaviour is determined by an imported code of conduct, as opposed to one's own free will and inner guidance. True integrity suggests that one refrains from wrongdoing not because of what others may think (if they found out), not because of the legal sanctions one might incur, not even because of social norms and mores, but because one is quite clear within oneself that it is the wrong thing to do. Or as C.S.Lewis was reputed to have said:

Integrity is doing the right thing even when no one is

watching.

Yet there is always someone watching and that person is you. So the question becomes not what the outside world will deem right or wrong, but what you determine is the right course of action at any point in time.

Bill Clinton's affair with Monica Lewinsky displayed no lack of integrity until he denied it. The denial was proof that he valued others' opinions over his own judgement and was prepared to be guided by them, not himself. He forsook his own frame of reference for an external one.

This self-referencing is key to Integrity - as soon as you promote external frames of reference over and above your inner one, your integrity is undermined. Perhaps the most common example of this is putting what others think ahead of what you think. That does not, for a moment, preclude listening to others and sincerely reflecting on alternative points of view - but these views need to be integrated by you if they are to be acted upon. Their view must become your view for it to guide you effectively.

Perhaps the aspect of entrepreneurship most challenged by this concept of integrity is competition. Considered a sine qua non of entrepreneurship, competition instantly breaks integrity simply because it requires your activities to be steered by those of others, whether or not you are in alignment with them.

Henry Ford articulates this well:

"Competition whose motive is merely to compete, to drive some other fellow out, never carries very far. The competitor to be feared is one who never bothers about you at all, but goes on making his own business better all the time."

Integrity then demands competition with yourself, not with others - within, not without.

I can personally attest to the huge relief this realisation affords anyone constantly looking over their shoulders at what the 'competition' may be doing. The second-guessing of others and the manic imagination over what they may be up to requires a lot of energy and inevitably evokes feelings of anxiety, fear and failure.

In terms of the theme of this book:

>Competition is Struggle

So if we eradicate competition with others, what replaces it? In 1910, Wallace Wattles published The Science of Getting Rich and wrote:

"You must get rid of the thought of competition. You are to create, not to compete for what is already created."

Creation is the antidote to competition and neatly aligns with previous insights regarding our basic human purpose, and the need to focus on process and activity rather than fixate on outcomes. Or as digital marketer and entrepreneur Neil Patel puts it:

"It's hard to beat your competition when you're copying them."

When you do copy them, success is far from guaranteed. In 2010, Microsoft attempted to turn their search engine noun: Bing, into a verb - just as Google had managed in 2006, but without any overt attempt. "Hey, Bing this!" failed to catch on, even with Microsoft's own employees. 12 years later, Google's global search market share was around 25 times that of Microsoft.

In 1968, a Russian Tu-144 made its maiden flight 2 months before the Anglo-French Concorde. The Russians had gone to great lengths to win this supersonic airliner race to the point, allegedly, of copying Concorde's design. Whether or not blueprints were stolen, the two aircraft bore an uncanny resemblance in general appearance and in many details. The Tu-144 was even dubbed Concordski.

In 1973 a Tu-144 took off at the Paris air show. The pilot vowed to outperform the Concorde prototype, which had just preceded it. Instead, it crashed, killing all on board and several on the ground. Another one crashed in 1979 and the Tu-144 was subsequently withdrawn from service.

Fortunately, most of us do not need to experience the endgame of slavish competition. Relinquishing the freedom of following your own path, in order to follow another's, creates a misalignment (a lack of integrity) that feels unpleasant enough for us to course-correct and get back on our own track of purpose and integrity. "To thine own self be true" is the foundation of integrity.

Integrity, in this expanded sense, needs to underpin your behaviour as an entrepreneur, not just for your own benefit but for that of the whole enterprise, through - as we'll explore shortly - its culture.

RESILIENCE

The second inner quality that supports the flow and expression of purpose is resilience. The capacity to bounce back, resilience is a non-negotiable attribute in the entrepreneurial world where adversity and resistance appear to be ever present.

Meaning literally *to jump back up again* - restoring mental and emotional equilibrium in the process - resilience mirrors the electron orbit metaphor for states of consciousness. In practice, the more conscious one is, the more resilient one becomes. Consciousness facilitates perception of things as they are, rather than as discerned through the mindset that we habitually (and less consciously) see things. The objective is not to dismantle the mindset, or even refine it, but simply to recognise that it is neither the observer nor the observed, instead creating that which the observer thinks they are observing.

We can think of mindset as a lens which distorts reality, or a belief-system which interprets it.

When a situation triggers a negative emotional state - always experienced as some form of lack or limitation - there is a sequence of events which takes place.

The situation creates a thought in mind such as: My client cannot pay the invoice. Mindset tells you that you won't be able to pay your bills as a result. Feelings of anxiety, fear, even shame or inadequacy follow. The feelings disable your capacity to take intelligent action - they swamp your mind.

In this scenario your mindset paints a picture of the future; one that is undesirable and creates debilitating feelings, compromising your ability to respond. The reality is that you do not know what the outcome will be. But you do know what you want. You also know that you can take intelligent action in support of a favourable outcome.

So a clear choice ensues between obsessing over unwanted outcomes, or using a favoured outcome to determine the next step in its support. This is to prioritise the imagination over the world of the senses.

Resilience stems from the ability to pay attention to what we want over and above the thoughts that often present themselves as 'reality'. It really boils down to maintaining attention or awareness on the present moment, in the face of a multitude of grim possibilities and bad memories that are aching to be dragged into the present.

So how do you achieve resilience? How do you maintain a balance that feels good whatever the situation, whilst maximising your chances of handling it for the optimal outcome?

The answer is simple and unsurprising: Practice

In this context, practice doesn't so much make perfect, as make permanent. Nor is it about creating habits, but rather dissolving them. It takes the form of two disciplines, one ongoing and ad hoc, the other scheduled. The first, to be practised whenever one remembers is commonly referred to and misunderstood as mindfulness. The second is meditation (see appendix 1), also widely misunderstood.

Both boost resilience because they respect the truth that nothing exists outside of the present moment - that infinitesimal (and infinite) snapshot of now. Of course, memories and fantasies exist in the now moment, but they are neither past nor future, simply artifices representing them - products of our minds.

Resilience thrives in the present moment because whatever has destabilised you has either now passed or is yet to be, if ever. Consciousness of now (which is the only true form of consciousness) renders anything else powerless to control you. You see it for what it is, simply a line, scene or act in the drama that you are witnessing. A drama that the entrepreneur can also write, direct and star in.

Anchored firmly in the present, it becomes increasingly difficult for circumstances to impact the way you feel, without your assent. Yet this is not about becoming less sensitive to your environment - quite the reverse - it amplifies your sensitivity but allows you a say in your feeling response, rather than being at the mercy of an emotional reaction. You have a choice over the impact it has upon you.

POSITIVITY

Positivity is generally understood to be the practice of being positive or optimistic in attitude. Yet the word positive originally had little to do with the concept of optimism. It derives from the Latin ponere - to place - meaning formally laid down, settled by agreement, hence certain.

Its opposing meaning to the word negative came much later. Only in the early 20th century did it evolve to carry the psychological sense of 'concentrating on what is constructive and good'. According to the Online Etymological Dictionary, Positive Thinking is attested from 1953.

Misunderstood, positivity can thwart the very thing it seeks, particularly so in its guise as positive thinking. Substituting the avalanche of negative thoughts that creates so much anxiety, stress and struggle in our lives, with an equal but opposite measure of 'positive', optimistic thoughts is to live in a fool's paradise.

This is the toxic positivity that Voltaire challenges in his satire Candide ou L'optimisme, in which the eponymous protagonist, Candide, inculcated with positivity by his mentor, Professor Pangloss, suffers a gradual disillusionment when his idyllic lifestyle takes a turn for the worse.

"All is for the best in the best of all possible worlds." - Pangloss' mantra seems totally at variance with Candide's lived experience.

Doubtless, a mind full of positive thoughts will prove more appealing than its converse. A positive attitude is more likely to get things done, in the face of opposition, than a negative one. Would you rather work with 'cup half full' people than eternal pessimists? Problems arise when the positivity becomes an intellectual activity, devoid of intelligence - a (Pan)glossy veneer hiding a sea of troubles.

The Daoist parable from the Mindset chapter reflects the optimal attitude for entrepreneurs to adopt. The farmer displays neither a positive nor a negative reaction to occurrences, responding with a non-committal 'maybe' whilst his neighbours oscillate between emotional extremes, predictably and relentlessly driven by the last event to unfold.

The emotional roller-coaster that this kind of unintelligent reaction creates is not just bad for the mental health of the entrepreneur, it also undermines the success of the enterprise and creates more struggle.

The trick is to hold any concept of positive or negative (good or bad) as lightly as possible, in the knowledge that these are no more than unconscious, intellectual judgements - fruits of the tree of knowledge of good and evil.

But, as we explore later on, the entrepreneur needs also to hold a vision in their imagination that remains untouched by the world as it presents itself. It becomes a certainty for them, indifferent to the slings and arrows of outrageous fortune. To be certain of a thing is to be positive of it. In this sense, positivity can never be toxic, if supported by an emotional resilience to events, and a clear goal held in the imagination.

Perhaps with this understanding of positivity as certainty, the Panglossian mantra becomes rather more pragmatic.

So, true positivity goes well beyond the mindless replacement of negative thoughts with positive ones, instead, the entrepreneur stays true to the desire, held firmly in the imagination as a vision, certain (positive) of its fulfilment.

Arnold Schwarzenegger's take on this is uncompromising:

"I hate Plan B," he said. "People perform better, in sports and everything else, if they don't have a Plan B. I've never, ever had a Plan B."

He continued: "I made a full commitment that I'm gonna go and be a bodybuilding champion, I made a full commitment that I'm gonna be in America, I made a full commitment that I'm gonna get into show business and I'm going to be a leading man, no matter what it takes I will do the work. I wanted to work over and over and over until I got it."

Sometimes, the gap between the vision and the status quo is so large, the entrepreneur attracts negativity, not support. Then it becomes all the more important to climb out of the purgatory of right and wrong, to dwell in the certainty of one's vision.

Opposites resist flow - positivity as certainty, expedites it.

Mindfulness

Mindfulness is the shortcut to accessing higher states of consciousness. It is brought about by focusing attention on the present - the now moment. The habitual state of consciousness for many of us is a mix of random perceptions of the world around us - courtesy of our five senses - and a stream of thoughts emanating from memory and imagination, conditioned by intellect and identity. This is a state of scattered attention in which little of note takes place. Sooner or later, life compels us to take constructive action which requires a higher degree of focus.

The practice of mindfulness is that of reconnecting with the present moment at every opportunity. It transcends the habits of mind, which can so easily prevail and hijack reality, including:

    Replaying in memory of past traumas

    Fantasising over unwanted outcomes

    Feeling shame for past events

    Regurgitating conflict with others

… and many more. In the present moment, the above have no reality and thus no impact.

Mindfulness is often described as the ability to control one's mind. However, in less expanded states of consciousness, this can often mean control by ego. Ego is a complex of ideas and beliefs that we invest our identity in. But as we have already explored, we are not the ideas and feelings we think we are. So ego as an identity is quite simply a mistake.

Some commentators on mindfulness advocate elimination of ego. This is also a mistake. Just as ideas, beliefs and opinions are an integral part of the human experience, so too is ego. As with any opinion, the question is not so much the quality of one's ego, as the degree to which one is identified with it. Put another way, is your ego directing your life, or are you?

Mindfulness expands consciousness, relegating ego to the rank of faithful servant, as opposed to overbearing master. As control of the mind is progressively relinquished (or quite suddenly in some cases), so it naturally becomes aligned with your deeper, purer and truer desires and aspirations.

Being mindful is being conscious. It demands vigilance and ongoing awareness of your inner dynamics, particularly the insidious indulgence in habits of mind that detract from the reality of who you are. But it does not require the kind of ego control that we all too easily try to apply to ourselves and those around us. Rather it is the clarity of mind that consciousness affords that steers our attention to where it is needed.

Ego-control of our minds is a struggle. Consciousness promotes flow.

Another important aspect of mindfulness is that it never promotes criticism, which is always and only the product of ego. Whether it is the overt character assassination of a colleague (usually behind their back and often masked as opinion or appraisal), or the silent inner judgement of another's behaviour, personality or character - criticism is destructive, not only of the target, but also of whoever is taking aim.

So-called constructive criticism is a clear exception to this rule - easily distinguished by the feelings and intent behind it, and immediately identifiable as positive and helpful rather than negative and damaging.

Refer to Appendix 1 for more on meditation. Although often mentioned in the same breath, meditation and mindfulness are distinct in practical terms. For instance, by all means drive your vehicle mindfully, but do not attempt meditation at the wheel!

Takeaways

- Expressing your purpose is a fundamental human urge
- Integrity lies in the process, not the outcome
- Competition is struggle - creativity is flow
- Resilience is found in the now, never the past or future
- Positivity as certainty is more useful than the opposite of negative
- True mindfulness anchors experience in the present

THE OUTER FLOW OF VISION

So far we've considered three aspects of entrepreneurship - purpose, integrity and resilience - which are all inner; that is, they are experienced within as an energetic complex of thought and feeling. And that is where they stay without a vehicle for expression - a context for action.

That vehicle is vision, which is an idealised image of what you want to create as a reality in your world. It is unmanifest - as soon as it becomes a reality, it ceases to be a vision. It is quite distinct from purpose, existing only in your imagination, and requiring a passage of time to come to fruition. Purpose, in contrast, expresses in the present, from moment to moment.

The creative force of purpose flows out, through vision, into the world of appearances - the creation.

Without a vision, there is no action, no flow and no thing is created. Vision is a prime responsibility of entrepreneurship, to the extent that whoever holds the clearest and most energetic vision of the enterprise is the de facto leader, regardless of title.

The essence of entrepreneurship is the transformation of a vision, held in the imagination, into a physical reality. Facilitating this process to optimise the chances of success requires a vision with several key attributes:

It needs to be inspirational. It needs to excite you with the energy, ambition and desire to achieve it.

It needs to be clear in your mind. It needs to have a mental form that you can recall with ease to nurture and develop.

It needs to be easily communicable. Entrepreneurship is never solitary - even solopreneurs have stakeholders that need to share and buy into the vision.

Finally, it needs to be treated as a living entity. Just as a child is conceived in the womb, developing to the point where it can be delivered, so your vision is conceived in your imagination and develops before being released into the world of form.

The practical, physical activities needed to give birth to your entrepreneurial vision are beyond the scope of this book. Thankfully, there are a multitude of resources to help the entrepreneur through the legal, financial and commercial challenges that await them.

But what of the metaphysical activities, those that take place in the theatre of the imagination? These have been the subject of study since the dawn of humanity. From

Buddhism to New Thought, from Theosophy to Quantum Mysticism, the notion that thoughts become things has entranced many who seek to make their ideas a physical reality. Yet many entrepreneurs that I have worked with, and possibly the great majority of the population remain oblivious to this dimension of activity.

Previously, we considered thought as being potentially more 'real' than things, on the basis that things - at least man-made things - could never exist without thought. Given creativity's relationship to thought, it makes sense to devote at least some time and energy to the development and incubation of the idea or vision, to maximise its chances of fruition.

What follows is a simple process to energise your vision to make it inspirational, clear and communicable. This process is nothing new and continues to be reiterated and refined by contemporary writers.

Sit quietly and comfortably, undisturbed. Close your eyes and bring into your imagination an appealing vision that you want to materialise in your life. This will be something that, as yet, does not exist, but something that, to you, is worthy, valuable and inspiring.

Imagine it not as it may be, but as it is. In other words, do not introduce the aspect of time into the vision. Remember that the vision in your imagination is at least as real as the physical form that it will create. So the vision is now - treat it as such.

See (create) whatever detail makes it come alive to you. You might envisage meetings, award ceremonies, bank balances, relationships, celebrations - all the fruits of your enterprise.

Take the positive emotions associated with the vision in all its glory and amplify them, bathe in them. Feel them as real, now.

Spend 5 minutes daily elaborating and nurturing your vision to make it as splendid, magnificent and inspirational as it can be in your imagination.

Perhaps the most important part of this process is the evoking of positive emotions. The way we feel determines our experience of life. When you bring to mind an old acquaintance, you may not remember a single word they said to you, but you will surely remember how you felt about them. Feelings also determine the decisions we make, so immersing ourselves in vibrant feelings can only enhance the way we act in the world.

Mysticism and Magic

Now we'll take a short excursion into the realms of mysticism and magic, without which any exploration of creativity and manifestation would be incomplete:

In many traditions and cultures across the globe there is mention of those who could rearrange creation purely through the power of thought, or at the very most, word. There are the mages, wizards, witches, magicians, all of whom could allegedly impact the physical, exclusively through non-physical intervention - some folk etymologies describe the meaning of the famous magic incantation: abracadabra, as "I will create as I speak".

Modern fantasy culture including the Marvel Universe, Game of Thrones and Harry Potter assign this power to some of their characters. The combined value of just these three franchises at over $100 billion suggests an enduring fascination with the power of thought, spoken or not.

All this begs the obvious question: can we get what we want purely through the creative power of thought, free from any need to act? Many ancient and modern sources affirm that you can - that unshakeable belief allied to focused attention on the object of desire must result in its manifestation.

However, many also recommend intelligent action in support of your creation.

Neville (Goddard), a key figure in the New Thought movement, tells a story of how in 1933 he travelled home for Christmas against all odds. He was telling his friend in New York how he had a strong desire to go see his family in Barbados, and how with no job or money it was not going to be possible.

"You are in Barbados." said his friend.

"I am in Barbados?" replied Neville.

He said, "Yes. You are now in Barbados. And so… you see Barbados, and you see America from Barbados, and you can smell the tropical land of Barbados, see only the little homes of Barbados, and that's all you do. You just simply sleep this night in Barbados."

Neville maintained this vision, even in the face of his own deep scepticism, for some time.

One morning the following letter arrived from his brother:

"I know you don't have a job, and there's no excuse for not coming. And so I'm enclosing a draft for fifty dollars… you may need a shirt, a pair of shoes, socks or something, and I've notified the Furness Withy Line that you'll come for a ticket. So the ticket is waiting for you at the Furness Line."

Significantly, Neville did not achieve his dream without taking action. Indeed, the money and ticket arrived unexpectedly and with no physical intervention on his part, but he still had to board the steamer to get to his destination.

In this example, the physical activity required to complete the manifestation only served to enhance the whole experience. Were he to have suddenly woken up in Barbados, having gone to sleep in New York, he might have been rather disappointed to miss out on sailing first-class, as he did.

So, whether it is possible or not - whether you believe in it or not - manifestation without action may well deny us experiences that are anything from simply enjoyable to life-changing. It is these experiences that provide us with opportunities to evolve in every dimension of our being.

I see this as being particularly so with entrepreneurship which can expose the entrepreneur to some of the most demanding, enlivening and exhilarating situations to be found in the world of work.

Hopefully we've established that as entrepreneurs we would not want to sit back, think thoughts and chant mantras in order to manifest our hearts' desires. And, that even if we could, the lack of action would deny us opportunities for new experiences, learning and growth - deny our participation in the full spectrum of human activity and diminish us as a consequence.

Now we need to explore two aspects of leadership that support the entrepreneur's outward flow of their vision:

CULTURE

The first of these is Culture. Deriving from the Latin colere: to tend, guard, till or cultivate, I think of organisational culture as collective behaviour. It's the way in which people, individually and collectively react or respond to events. The entrepreneur's obligation is to cultivate and support a climate that promotes the optimal response to whatever happens. This responsibility has two dimensions.

Firstly, a prime responsibility of the entrepreneur is that of creating, protecting and nurturing the environment in which the enterprise develops. The physical, built environment includes the resources required by each member of the team. It's tempting to aspire to accepted norms: a bright, spacious, air-conditioned environment, kept clean and tidy, with a local travel network and amenities. However, the financial realities of early stage entrepreneurship frequently prohibit such luxury.

The first startup I worked for featured a mezzanine room within an industrial unit with no natural daylight and a propensity to reach sauna-like temperatures in summer. Tucked away in a remote industrial estate with no public transport, the enterprise lacked many creature comforts. Yet, the vibrant culture - brimming with energy, ambition and excitement - rendered these drawbacks insignificant. Moreover, the directors took every effort to provide all that was required, including a continuous supply of cakes and biscuits, regular meals out, and highly flexible working hours. They wisely considered these perquisites as investments with a high return.

The established criteria for the ideal working environment have recently been shredded by the arrival of covid - and the traditional demarcation between home and office, overturned by lockdowns. The world of work is still trying to find a post-covid equilibrium that satisfies both the needs of the organisation and the benefits of working from home (WFH).

Like many other contemporary issues, the WFH question has polarised opinion. Some employers have issued unilateral directives to work from the office 5 days a week. Others have sold their premises in favour of exclusively working from home.

Many working in healthcare, manufacturing and hospitality do not have a WFH option. For those that do, the burning question is: how does WFH impact productivity? Are workers more efficient at work or at home? At the time of writing, the debate rages with studies supporting both ends of the spectrum and everything between.

In the absence of definitive data resolving the issue once and for all - something that appears unlikely even in the long term - I would counsel employers that can, to consult with staff, experiment, review and refine their approach to WFH over time, eschewing principle, 'best practice' and others' opinions in favour of empirical data. However, we must accept that this can be a highly charged and emotive subject for some. It may even be necessary to ultimately enforce a rule that will lead to some of your people deciding to leave. It is unsurprising that the adjustments we have all made in response to the turmoil of lockdown will have changed some of our priorities.

Secondly - over and above a positive physical environment - is the need for a behavioural ambience which enables stakeholders in the enterprise to feel safe, valued and empowered. This responsibility of the entrepreneur is rather more subtle to grasp and can easily trump the benefits of a supportive physical environment.

In contrast to my early startup experience, later on in my career I witnessed a very different approach to corporate culture. The company in question, a wholly owned subsidiary of a global technology business, wanted for nothing, providing comfortable offices, good salaries and business-class international travel. One day the UK sales director decided to implement a clean-desk policy, having presumably read the latest organisational development theory in the Harvard Business Review, or some such font of wisdom. He issued an edict that all desks were to be free of paper by 5.30pm each day.

Within a week, everyone had established the admirable, daily habit of clearing their desks by close of play. Everyone, that was, except Brian. Brian, our technician, had amassed, over the years, metre-high stacks of technical journals, papers and manuals, all precariously balanced near the edges of his desk, leaving just enough room for a keyboard and monitor. Unfortunately for Brian, the relative neatness of other desks made the state of his all the more prominent. One day in Brian's absence, the sales director decided to implement his policy on Brian's behalf, moving the stacks to another location. On returning, instead of thanking his boss, Brian had a full-blown panic attack, promised his resignation and walked out.

What our progressive director had omitted to take into account was not so much that Brian was neurodiverse (a description that did not exist at the time) and very attached to the apparent disorder on his desk, but that we're all different and what may float one person's boat will sink another. A safe, empowering environment for one employee may be quite the reverse for another.

Culture needs to promote and fulfil everyone's urge to express their purpose through a collective vision. Applying strictures to it requires intelligence and minimalism. Too much structure is just as problematic as not enough. There is no formula for prescribing the sweet spot between order and chaos - the entrepreneur needs to acquire the awareness and sensitivity to find it themselves.

The key determinant of a company's behavioural culture is easily missed, even by the most outwardly successful and revered leaders. This anecdote illustrates it:

An entrepreneur is lamenting to her coach how invisible she seems to be and how little influence she seems to wield. The coach tells her that the session is over and hands her an invoice, adding: "But before we meet next, I want you to buy a copy of Time magazine and carry it with you wherever you go".

At the next meeting the entrepreneur continues to complain that nothing has changed and that her presence seems to go unnoticed. At this point the coach pauses and holds an uncomfortable silence. Eventually the entrepreneur remarks: "but there is one funny thing - everyone seems to have started reading Time magazine".

The entrepreneur - the holder of the vision - is the single most influential individual in any enterprise, with everyone looking to them for guidance, to a greater or lesser extent. The way they behave will influence how those around them behave - and that's not to say that others will necessarily emulate the behaviour, but it will certainly modify their own.

So how should an entrepreneur behave? Referring back to our exploration of integrity, the answer to this question has to come from within - any application of a set code breaks integrity and renders the entrepreneur a victim of whatever theory they have last been exposed to, rather than the architect of intelligent, conscious behaviour, appropriate to the situation.

Most of the entrepreneurs I've worked with might loosely be described as 'good eggs' - well-intentioned, of good character, pleasant, agreeable and nice to work with. Few have been ego-driven, overbearing tyrants, running roughshod over people and their feelings. Yet niceness has been no guarantee of success - far from it.

In this respect the ruthless boss may have a great advantage, addressing difficult issues with more gusto than the day-to-day. The 'nice' boss, often subliminally motivated by the need to be liked, prefers to avoid confrontation by finding good (but spurious) reasons to defer it. What the entrepreneur doesn't do is just as influential as what they do. The failure to engage can have disastrous consequences.

Several of my clients have put both their mental and physical wellbeing - as well as the survival of the business - at severe risk by failing to confront the adverse behaviour of employees that have 'gone rogue'. Such has been their reluctance to 'grasp the nettle' that the behaviours had become normalised and entrenched over the years, to the point where they had effectively seized power and were calling the shots in place of the rightful leader.

In each case, the only possible course of action was to remove the offending individual and terminate their employment, which they did with my help. Yet this was as difficult for the entrepreneur as it was obvious, and was only made possible through close support.

To ignore or tolerate negative behaviour is not only to support it, but to actively condone it and become complicit in it. The inevitable sense of struggle that this will incur is amplified each time action is postponed.

•

A key determinant of culture is recruitment. Each new hire will impact culture to some degree. Yet many entrepreneurs assume - often without giving the matter any consideration at all - that each new arrival will adopt and conform to the prevailing culture thereby strengthening it.

Corporates betray a similar ignorance by attempting to influence culture through the use of values and culture statements. Posted on walls and screen savers, the architects of these initiatives - usually the senior leadership or c-suite team - seem oblivious to the real drivers of culture, which are far closer to home.

Recruitment is a high-risk business. Whatever measure the enterprise takes to minimise that risk, the reality is that you will not find out whether the hire is a good fit or not, before it's too late - probably months into the contract. Making the process more elaborate and sophisticated is not the way to go.

My son recently told me how he had been asked to deliver a video cv in a job application. He had immediately rejected the opportunity on the grounds that it was an unnecessary complication to the process that revealed the insecurities of a business that he wanted no involvement in.

Some companies involve multiple stakeholders requiring several interviews. Some request business plans for strategic initiatives which they no doubt benefit from whether or not the applicant is hired.

David Leithead, chief operations manager of Morgan McKinley UK, tells HR Magazine that a lack of clarity, both internally and when speaking to candidates, can slow down recruitment.

"The involvement of multiple stakeholders inevitably causes the hiring process to increase in length, but is often deemed a necessity to ensure the right hire is made," he said.

"When a process is vague, the timetable drifts, or a hiring organisation is not transparent about other applicants – particularly internal – being in play, jobseekers will often quickly lose engagement and interest."

With the exception of some highly specialised roles, recruitment needs to be brief and focused. Risk does not arise from the simplicity of the process, but from a lack of hiring clarity. The cv tells you what the applicant can do. The interview reveals how they do it and their potential for growth.

We can crudely but effectively divide a candidate's appeal into two aspects - ability and attitude. Many hirers fixate on the former, being a variable that can be reduced to a series of bullet points or tick boxes; the latter cannot. Unsurprisingly, most hires fail because of attitude, not aptitude - so the balance of focus needs to shift, prioritising attitude over ability.

Some years ago I interviewed a foreign national for a technical role. He met all our criteria and seemed to have the right attitude too. I was left with a feeling of unease which I couldn't put my finger on. In reception, I got chatting to him waiting for his taxi. He seemed far more relaxed and voluble, eventually betraying a prejudicial attitude to a minority group that would have caused havoc in the business. My unease was well-founded and, needless to say, he was not hired.

This anecdote illustrates both the criticality of attitude and the need for a relaxed environment over an intentionally stressed one. As hirers, we need to determine how people will behave in the working environment, not an interview environment. Unless the working ambient is one of intensity and pressure, we need to do everything possible to put the candidate at their ease - not out of kindness, but in the knowledge that they are more likely to unveil themselves in a conducive setting.

On several occasions, I've noticed how interviewers can seem less relaxed than the interviewee. This is not helpful. Only those that can create an atmosphere of calm assurance should interview.

Finally, the number of interviewers on the panel needs to be proportionate. Anymore than two, three as a maximum, displays a corporate insecurity which should be a red flag to any candidate.

Remember that for the type of person you want to hire, they will be assessing you every bit as much as you are assessing them.

Delegation

The second aspect of leadership crucial to the realisation of one's vision is delegation.

Delegation is a cornerstone of leadership without which no organisation can thrive. In fact it's a bit of a no-brainer - if you don't pass tasks on to someone else, you'll burn out whilst those around you twiddle their thumbs.

It's so obvious, why wouldn't you delegate as much as you possibly can to your team? It's the only way that a business can scale effectively.

So it may come as some surprise that many of the leaders that I have worked with, whilst knowing exactly how, why, what and to whom to delegate, frequently get it so wrong.

To find out why this syndrome is endemic in many organisations, let's take a look at the word delegate, which comes from the Latin *legare* meaning to send with a commission. The prefix de- means away from, so to delegate means to send someone away with a task. The act of sending away is critical here - it used to mean that the delegate was isolated and incommunicado, with no recourse to whoever sent them. Therefore they had to carry a degree of autonomy, responsibility and authority to get the job done - they couldn't just turn up and say: "hang on, I'll ask my boss."

Today there is no isolation and we have 24/7 connectivity with colleagues. The same technology that brings us so many benefits, also subconsciously encourages leaders to delegate the task, but without the responsibility that would once have been taken for granted. Instead of being compelled to invest trust in the delegate, the leader can keep tabs on progress from moment to moment, questioning, assessing, intervening and directing at will. This withholding of responsibility is both insidious and pernicious and often takes place initially with neither the delegator, nor the delegate being fully aware of it.

Micromanagement is the bane of teams led by those who will not or cannot invest trust in their people. All too frequently, managers are quick to confide in others that they cannot trust certain members of the team to get their jobs done. Which begs the question:

Why are you employing people you cannot trust?

My observation is that far from retaining untrustworthy employees, managers project the lack of trust they have in themselves on others. Just as in many other scenarios, the workplace becomes a mirror for our inner worlds of thinking, feeling and perception.

The implications of delegating tasks without full responsibility, accountability and authority are broad:

When a manager withholds accountability for the delegated task, it demeans the delegate, depriving them of the opportunity to learn and grow - relegating them to the status of a menial automaton. Over time, the manager will attract those that need constant supervision, whilst repelling those that want to uncover their potential, to be the best they can be.

Furthermore, the manager deprives themself of the same opportunities, prioritising the need to constantly monitor delegated activities amongst more and more staff. This is a root cause of poor performance and productivity, let alone stress, burnout, conflict and anxiety. There are well-proven links between long term anxiety and clinical depression - the prognosis for mental health, in this context, is not a good one.

So the challenge for all of us as leaders is to delegate not just the task in hand, but also the full responsibility that goes with it. How do you do it?

Firstly, you need to be certain that each and every member of your team is up to the responsibilities you need to place on them. If they aren't, you either train them, or change them. Doing nothing is not an option.

Secondly, when you interact with any member of your team, see them as humans with potential far beyond what you or they may perceive - don't let your biases, impressions and mindsets diminish them in any way. You cannot deprecate another without deprecating yourself. Remember that good leaders get people to do things they didn't think were possible.

Thirdly, when it comes to delegation, invest full trust in them to the point where you can walk away and forget about the task you have delegated, however uncomfortable that may be, at first. Replace apprehension with trust. If you sincerely cannot do this, you have no business running an enterprise.

Finally, if results appear sub-optimal, you will have plenty of data available to increase the chances of the desired outcome next time around. The opportunities for development, both for you and those involved, are inestimable.

A key tenet of leadership that supports good delegation is:

> You are not responsible for your people

This often comes as a surprise even to seasoned managers. The reason why this always holds true - at least for functioning adults - is that they are responsible for themselves and their behaviour. We are each responsible for our lives, our speech and actions - no one else. The leader is responsible purely for creating an environment in which everyone can grow in their capacity to take on new and exciting responsibilities.

A common objection to this truism is that a manager should not 'throw anyone under the bus' by publicly blaming them when they get something wrong. This is absolutely correct. The manager takes collective responsibility for the team or organisation in relation to those outside of it. But within her team, individual responsibility prevails.

Give responsibility whenever you can and your delegation will unleash everyone's potential, including your own.

Delegation of task and responsibility is not always benign. I have witnessed at least two instances of leaders wilfully setting their delegates up for failure by withholding either critical resources or information, stepping back and waiting for disaster. They could not be accused of interference or micromanagement, just a malign desire to prove the delegates unequal to the challenge.

Extraordinary as this may seem, in both cases the motivation behind the deliberate sabotage was simply to reinforce their sense of superiority in order to compensate for an inner crisis of inferiority. It worked, temporarily.

TAKEAWAYS

- Vision is the idealised, inspirational image of what you are working to create

- Realising your vision starts in the mind - in your imagination

- Culture - collective behaviour - is needed to support your vision becoming real

- Delegation delegates responsibility, not just task and resource

- You are not responsible for any other adult but you

TIME AND MONEY

'Time is money' goes the old saying - and you can certainly buy time with money, just as you can accumulate money over time. There is an equivalence that connects them even though they manifest very differently.

Both are abstract concepts that need the familiar to represent them. Time is typically depicted as a hand rotating across a clock face; money, as a piece of paper or a coin. Today, both are alternatively represented as digits and units.

But any similarities are dwarfed by the fundamental difference that time is the fourth dimension of physical reality, without which space could not exist, whilst money is a relatively recent introduction that has no influence beyond the sphere of human activity.

So why bring them together in the same chapter? In working with a variety of entrepreneurs, time and money are the two parameters that come under the most scrutiny. In this context, they are inextricably intertwined: if you run out of time, you will run out of money; if you run out of money, the enterprise will run out of time.

They are also the two commodities that, when in lack, appear to generate the most struggle and the least sense of flow.

Flow is intrinsic to both time and money - without flow, neither has any utility. Happily, we cannot influence the flow of time - at least objective time. We can, and do, interfere with the flow of money, the implications of which we explore below.

The shared characteristics of time and money will allow us to use time as an exemplar for an approach to money that will help shift the financial struggles that many entrepreneurs experience.

TIME AND TIDE

"Time and tide wait for no man" is a quote of uncertain origin that confirms time as an immutable pillar of creation.

Just as the incoming tide was oblivious to King Canute's command to halt, and not wet his feet and robes, so time continues to flow at the rate of exactly one second per second, resistant to any attempts to tamper with it.* However, the comparison with tide - the periodic movement of the oceans generated by the moon as it orbits the earth - introduces a key aspect of our experience of time which is neatly illustrated by Brutus in Shakespeare's play Julius

Caesar:

> There is a tide in the affairs of men.
> Which, taken at the flood, leads on to fortune;
> Omitted, all the voyage of their life
> Is bound in shallows and in miseries.
> On such a full sea are we now afloat,
> And we must take the current when it serves,
> Or lose our ventures.

The tide is used as a metaphor for the ebb and flood which takes place in human affairs, of which business is an integral, perhaps dominant part. Timing, not just time, becomes the critical element.

When is the time right? Do we sit and wait for the perfect moment before riding the wave? This is exactly what surfers do - they wait for a suitable wave and then position themselves to ride it. But here's the thing, they don't wait on the beach where they would see the wave and surely miss it - they wait in the water. They are already in business.

Waiting for the time to be right can put the entrepreneur into a state of suspended animation, awaiting a moment that never comes. Waiting to have enough savings to leave your employment; waiting for an upturn in the economy; waiting to recruit the right person.

This is not to urge anyone to throw caution to the wind and dive into deep waters without preparation. What it does encourage is activity in support of your goals, whether or not you think you are in a position to commit everything to them right now. Then, when the time is right, you are ready to 'take it at the flood'.

Amazon may not have become the world's largest online retailer quite so seamlessly without first having established itself as an online bookseller.

At a more familiar level, the would-be entrepreneur and the solopreneur can always take steps right now in pursuit of their vision, regardless of circumstances. Until they do, they will never be in a position to ride a wave when it comes along.

In terms of concepts visited in previous chapters, our purpose can and should be deployed now, however remote or invisible the realisation of our vision may be. The latin motto carpe diem - seize the day - applies to the beginning of the journey, not its fulfilment. The start is now under your complete control, the end is not.

Unless you are already in the business of your purpose - in the water - you will be 'bound in shallows and in miseries', until such time as you start taking even the smallest action in that direction.

* This of course only holds true for those of us who do not travel at speeds approaching that of light. If you're a photon, you have not aged one second in 13.7 billion years.

A Persistent Illusion

Albert Einstein was reputed to have written: "the distinction between past, present, and future is only a stubbornly persistent illusion." which is tantamount to stating that time does not exist.

In 1908, the British philosopher J.M.E. McTaggart wrote a paper entitled 'The Unreality of Time' in which he states: "Time must be rejected, not because it cannot be explained, but because the contradiction cannot be removed." McTaggart changed his reason for the rejection of time in a later publication, but the conclusion remained the same.

Here we use some much simplified logic to expose the possibility of paradox, if not contradiction:

We can say with certainty (and due respect of tense) that the past does not exist, just as we can say that neither does the future. The past used to exist, but not now. The future will exist, but not now. In other words, neither the past nor the future are real. One was, the other will be, but neither are.

So if time is the movement from the past to the future, neither of which exist, we can surely claim that time has, at the very least, a rather shaky foundation.

The only element of time that appears to exist is the present - the now.

Whether or not the past and future have any reality now, they are measurable: the past being at least 13.7 billion years old and the future at least 22 billion years, according to the latest astrophysical research. But the present, being an infinitesimally brief snapshot of time, has zero duration when compared to past and future. In the context of past and future, the present does not exist.

We could also say that, from the point of view of the now, the present is infinitely long - because we are always in the present - with past and future having no meaning or reality.

It all depends on our frame of reference: if we reference the past, the present is a fleeting moment - so small as to be possibly non-existent. If we reference the now, it is eternal.

Our perception of time is warped by the past. We mistake memories of the past for the past itself. Memories are constructs of the past, never what actually was. The only reality is the ever-present, infinite now.

So what are the practical implications of this metaphysical whimsy? Quite simply, the more rooted in the present you are, the more time you have - the less distracted you will be by thoughts, memories and events. You also become less susceptible to habits of your mind telling you that, amongst many other things, you do not have enough time.

The way we experience time is through change. Unless one moment is different from the next, there can be no perception of time. Because change is intrinsic to the physical universe, in which every thing is in motion, time is woven into the fabric of creation, as is space.

The experience of time and its dependency on change (or possibly vice versa) operates at a psychological level too. We can sit still with our eyes shut and still sense it - usually by getting bored and wanting a different (changed) experience. Our feelings are never static - emotions are so called for good reason, being ever in motion.

But in deep meditation, time becomes less apparent and can fade away altogether. This is said to be because all we are left with is consciousness or being, neither of which are subject to change and thus beyond space and time.

There is widespread agreement amongst those that practise mindfulness and meditation that the elevated state of consciousness that one enters creates a timefulness which gets things done more efficiently, more potently and more joyfully. It also manages to dispense with many things that don't need doing. There is a flow to it.

Time management becomes redundant when you address the real reasons behind an apparent shortage of time. Elevated states of consciousness promote a clear and quiet mind which easily selects what to do and what to leave undone. There is no need to import and rely on external time management rules and disciplines, many of which take time to execute and often feel both unnatural and unsustainable, as do many remedies that address symptoms, not causes.

Just as we recognise that time is objectively a constant, we also know, all too well, that subjective time is non-linear. Einstein explained this to his secretary with the following quip:

"An hour sitting with a pretty girl on a park bench passes like a minute, but a minute sitting on a hot stove seems like an hour." Time flows when you're having fun.

Do What You Want

No one of sound mind would opt to sit on a hot stove, yet many of us choose to spend our time doing things which, although not quite as overtly uncomfortable, take their toll on our psychological and physical welfare over time.

This leads us on to one of the most significant guiding principles of entrepreneurship:

> Do what you really want

In my last book, The Broken CEO, I explain in detail why this statement - an apparent recipe for rampant hedonism - is, in reality, the only formula for true success. The only true way of knowing whether you are doing what you want is through how it feels. This relates not just to action, but also to speech and thought. So we can express a corollary of this rule as:

> If it doesn't feel good, don't do it!

Some of us would have had a far easier and more pleasant life to date observing this guidance rather than trying to push, struggle and force our way through the difficulties we encounter - many of which are pleading with us to stop.

I recall an early entrepreneurial endeavour marketing Italian-manufactured, plastic extrusions to various UK markets. It made perfect sense from a logistical, cultural and business point of view: I am familiar with the Italian language and business culture; I had good links with the supplier and I had plenty of b2b marketing experience. But the problem - only clearly visible with the benefit of hindsight - was that the venture did not inspire me. The business vision was perfectly laudable but was not aligned with my purpose. In other words, my heart wasn't in it.

What should have been a relatively easy way of making money by creating new supply chains, turned into an unrewarding grind, mirrored perfectly by a lack of commercial traction. At the time, I put this down to the market. Now, I see it simply as a natural result of doing something that I didn't really want to do.

Significantly, if the venture had been financially successful, it would have just prolonged the agony of the dissonance between my purpose and vision. You might call this compassionate failure!

But, in applying this maxim, how will you avoid a life of superficial pleasure-seeking, on the one hand - and how will you know when to engage with seemingly insurmountable challenges on the other?

In the early 1900s, Aleister Crowley founded Thelema - a western esoteric movement whose motto was: *Do what thou wilt shall be the whole of the Law.* Crowley went on to become a notorious icon of hedonistic gratification - judged a libertine at best, a depraved monster at worst.

In happy contrast, Saint Augustine, Bishop of Hippo and paragon of virtue, also enjoined us to: *Love and do what thou wilt.* Perhaps the addition of the word love explains the vast gulf between the lives these two men led.

Augustine also said: "Let us leave a little room for reflection in our lives, room too for silence. Let us look within ourselves and see whether there is some delightful hidden place inside where we can be free of noise and argument." It is exactly in this state that what you really want becomes clear.

At this point I will reassert one of the central tenets of this book:

The feeling of happiness, contentment and fulfilment, together with a state of clarity, peace and positivity, are the causes of success, not the results. They are success. They are the beginning and the end. They are not contingent, they are chosen.

Their dependency on circumstance is an illusion of our own creation. To pursue them as the outcome of some worldly activity, result or success is to demean them and render us immune to their power to transform our life experience from struggle to flow - from failure to success.

The realisation that the way we feel is independent of circumstance liberates us to follow our innermost desires, irrespective of outward appearances.

Money Money Money

The essence of money is energy. Money gets things done, moves things. According to the musical Cabaret, it makes the world go round. If you were to remove it from our current civilisation, society might well collapse overnight. Yet it has no intrinsic value, it is purely symbolic, a means of exchange - exchanging the energy expended by one party, for that of another.

For all its neutrality - money has no agenda, no memory - it is both reviled and adored in seemingly equal measure. How many times have we heard that:

- Money is the root of all evil (originally, the love of money is the root of all evil)
- The best things in life are free
- Money can't buy you love

The biblical term, filthy lucre, confirms money's sordid status in some quarters. Yet why should such an essential commodity attract anything other than desire, appreciation and gratitude? Perhaps it is easier for some of us to disparage money than to admit to its lack, just as the fox in Aesop's fable claimed that the grapes were sour, simply because he could not reach them. As a necessary evil, its utility is grudgingly accepted and hence its lack becomes justifiable.

Today, money is essential for the vast majority of us. As a need it is not dissimilar to air and water. Without your own money, or someone else's, life soon becomes unsustainable. The sadhus of India who renounce all earthly attachments - including money - maintain their basic needs through the charity of others who do rely on money.

As essential as it is, many of us - entrepreneurs included - experience a lack of money, not an abundance. Its lack seems to prevent us from following St. Augustine's injunction to 'do what thou wilt', cramping our style and restricting our options.

So how do we entrepreneurs reconcile the need for money with its apparent scarcity?

To answer this critical question, let's consider a synonym for money: currency. Originally indicating the condition of flowing - as in a water current or electric current - it has the same root as the Italian word *correre*, meaning to run. Movement, or flow, is intrinsic to money. This is borne out by the simple fact that money in a safe or pocket has no value until it is spent. Its impact, value and energy only manifest when it is being exchanged - when it is flowing from one party to another. If you stop the flow, the money ceases to have any utility.

In this respect, the flow or current of money mirrors the flow of subjective time. If we choose to do too little with our time, opportunities are missed, boredom ensues, change is suspended and our experience of life goes on hold. Paradoxically, this state is often accompanied by a sense of being time-poor, experienced as time passing too quickly for comfort.

So, just as we entrepreneurs should never wait to get started, so should we immediately establish a flow of energy, in the form of money, in support of our enterprise. As blindingly obvious as this may seem, our money (and time) mindsets can make it as difficult as it is true.

Money Mindsets

Our attitudes to money present many of us with the biggest challenges we have in our entrepreneurial lives. Some hide in plain sight as 'common sense' and others hover subliminally, under the radar.

Perhaps the most established is the belief that money is limited in supply, epitomised by the old adage: money doesn't grow on trees - even though much of it is still made from paper! This may or may not hold true at the macro-economic scale (which is beyond the scope of this book), but at the personal level, the fallacy is easy to demonstrate: According to the Bank for International Settlements, trading in foreign exchange markets reached $6.6 trillion per day in April of 2019. That equates to over two thousand, trillion dollars per year and excludes the money flowing within each currency domain. That's a lot of current!

The next mindset that trips us up is the belief that 'everything will be ok when I have the money I need'. This leads us to creating and tolerating all kinds of privations, pending the arrival of the life-changing sum. The issue with this mindset is the belief that, right now, everything is not ok and that you have to experience lack and limitation pending the abundance you yearn for.

What we focus on, and the meaning we give it, creates our reality. So whatever we might aspire to at some point in the future will be rewritten by the stories we tell of the present.

This is the real essence of the law of attraction which will deliver more of what we really believe about the here and now. If we perceive lack and believe in it, that is our experience. If we see and believe the abundance around us, that is what we experience. Free will gives us the option to choose.

To achieve this kind of freedom, we need to disconnect the way we feel from the appearance of the circumstances we find ourselves in, as explored in the mindfulness chapter. But rather than cite tired and moot examples of how you can be happy with little money, it may be more edifying to consider the opposite.

The psychologist, Bob Kenny, one of the architects of a Boston College survey of the very rich said: "Sometimes I think that the only people in this country who worry more about money than the poor are the very wealthy. They worry about losing it, they worry about how it's invested, they worry about the effect it's going to have. And as the zeroes increase, the dilemmas get bigger."

I have heard many anecdotes from those connected with ultra-high net worth individuals that, although extreme wealth solves a bunch of problems, it presents plenty more in place.

The conclusion I draw from this is that whilst money can seem to make you happy, it can also appear to cause unhappiness. So, money being neutral, its emotional impact is wholly down to the individual and how they choose to respond or react to it. Nothing to do with the money itself.

Interestingly, Kenny also says that most wealthy people eventually discover the satisfactions of philanthropy and that the experience of giving away their wealth - in addition to being pleasurable and empowering - also helps teach the donor that money can be a burden, harming or unsettling a recipient if given without caution. Philanthropic activity respects money's need to flow.

Restricting the movement of money is the result of grasping and trying to hold on to it, violating its fluidity. At its limit, the miser becomes financially constipated, amassing as much as possible and discharging as little as he can get away with. At the other extreme, unregulated flow causes the spendthrift to deplete reserves faster than they can be replenished - a form of incontinence. Both are best avoided.

So what are the practical upshots of these financial insights?

Firstly, money - being energy - is likely to be an indispensable means to realising your vision. But it makes a self-sabotaging end in itself. It is a great servant, an awful master. Don't seek to accrue it, other than for purchasing big-ticket items. Instead, allow it to flow.

Secondly, acknowledge and appreciate the fact that, in all likelihood, you have more than enough money, right now, to take some action, however small, in pursuit of your dream. If your vision is to buy and live in a palace, but you don't have the funds to do it now, you likely have enough to spend a couple of days in one. Do it.

Thirdly, whenever, and as soon as you catch yourself lamenting a shortage of money (or any other commodity, for that matter) remind yourself that you have enough right now to do what you need. Practise feeling how you want to feel, regardless of appearances.

Finally, love it, appreciate it and be grateful for it, always remembering that it is a neutral symbol of energy, that only has value when it flows.

The application of this approach to funding your enterprise is fundamental. There are countless sources from which money can arrive at your disposal, beyond loans and investments. Make sure that you are open to all of them in principle, without even knowing what they might be.

A couple of years ago, a longstanding friend of mine took a flight from London to Los Angeles en route to an alternative medicine centre in Mexico, specialising in cancer cures.

Having tried every possible alternative therapy he could find, he had decided to spend his remaining funds on a last ditch attempt to beat his terminal prognosis.

At the Heathrow checkin desk, he was asked if he would change seat to accommodate a mix-up with the seat allocation. He agreed and found himself onboard, chatting to a very attentive and somewhat mysterious woman in the seat next to him. They briefly exchanged their stories before she asked him the purpose of his trip. He willingly explained in detail and made no bones of the fact that the trip would all but empty his bank account, but given the nature of his illness, it was not of so much concern.

Towards the end of the flight, the woman told him she wanted to make a donation and asked him for his bank details. My friend, although bemused, was touched by the suggestion and having gained the impression that the woman had means, was happy to give them, thinking nothing more of it.

Arriving in Mexico the following day, he remembered his conversation with his fellow passenger and logged into his bank account online. To his total astonishment, he discovered that she had transferred the sum of £24,000. Initially he was sceptical but after calling his bank, was eventually assured that the money had been transferred, that there had been no mistake and that it was now his to do with what he wished.

Sadly, my friend is no longer with us, the cancer got the better of him not long after his trip. But his story provides us with some powerful insights into the flow of money.

Firstly, he offered no resistance to the flow of events: having his seat changed; answering his benefactor's questions; giving her his bank details. If he had avoided just one of those, the story would have been very different.

Secondly, he was certainly not expecting a sum of that magnitude. But, what he did expect was that, even though he was about to run out of money, everything would be ok - he had more fear of the cancer than of being penniless.

Thirdly, he allowed what money he did have to flow where he wanted it. He did not stop the flow on the basis that the money might be needed for something else. If he had decided not to go, he would never have sat next to the mysterious passenger and benefited from her philanthropy.

This modern parable illustrates an approach to funding which is far more organic and less constrained by convention than the received wisdom. It reminds us to focus on what we want and to discount every argument - however practical and reasonable - that tells us we can't have it.

All too often, the struggle entrepreneurs experience in the process of trying to source funds is down to assuming where the money will come from, whilst subconsciously blocking it from alternative sources.

TAKEAWAYS

- Time and money need to flow
- Time and money are neutral
- Don't wait - start now
- Stay present
- Do what you want and…
- …let money flow in support of it
- You attract more of what you are

SUCCESS GUARANTEED

Am I claiming to provide you with a guaranteed means of achieving success? The short answer is: yes. Unsurprisingly perhaps, the longer answer includes a few caveats…

The first qualification is about success itself. What is it? In entrepreneurial terms, it's often cited as a growing business that makes money, provides employment and delivers a product or service that people want and appreciate.

That used to sound perfectly reasonable to me until I encountered the scores of entrepreneurs, business owners and CEOs that had achieved all of that and more, whilst concurrently experiencing struggle, deep dissatisfaction, fear and insecurity, in some cases manifesting as serious mental illness - not the kind of success that I would aspire to.

The word success derives from the Latin for outcome. What is the outcome that entrepreneurs desire? Is it a thriving business or is it a sense of completeness and freedom? I would suggest that without the latter, the former is meaningless. Yet many of us embark on an entrepreneurial journey believing that the business itself will give us what we crave. It doesn't because it can't. Only we can do that.

In this respect, businesses are no different from relationships. If we go into a relationship expecting it to complete us, it eventually ends up disappointing both parties. If your 'other half' decides to be someone else's other half, where does that leave you - can you survive as half a person? Yet if we form a relationship from an established feeling of wholeness, it can provide us with even more than we expected.

I am not suggesting that we need to be feeling happy and complete before starting an enterprise - rather that we do well to derive that sense of wholeness from ourselves (the only source it can come from), not from our activity in the world, or another person.

The nature of worldly enterprise is cyclical - it has ups and downs, ebbs and flows. As soon as you pin your emotional wellbeing on these movements, you subject yourself to an ongoing fairground ride that will wear you down, regardless of the 'success' of the venture.

The second qualification is the need to respect the symmetry between business development and personal development. An enterprise is the creation of the entrepreneur and is made - knowingly or not - in their image. Unless the entrepreneur mirrors this growth in terms of their own personal development, the venture will plateau prematurely and encounter overwhelming difficulties that the entrepreneur is hard-pressed to overcome. Struggle ensues as the venture outgrows its creator.

The final caveat is that of the mutable nature of outcome. The inner growth that entrepreneurs experience on their entrepreneurial journey means they are different people now than when they started. So the vision that inspired them to conceive the business may not inspire them to progress it beyond a certain point. Entrepreneurs that cash out early on in the growth cycle have not necessarily missed an opportunity or failed - they may simply have evolved their vision or purpose well beyond whatever got them started.

What follows in this chapter is a very plastic approach to entrepreneurial success, in the terms described above.

In The Beginning

Any enterprise, however grand or mundane, is first experienced as an idea, emerging in mind. If the attendant feeling resonates with you, it attracts more attention and becomes an urge. At this point you have an idea providing direction and an impulse supplying the energy for action. The idea is a fledgling vision, the urge is your purpose seeking expression.

The idea is a concept, conceived in your imagination. This process is not dissimilar to that of procreation - an egg is fertilised and takes on a life of its own. As you give the idea your attention, it grows to the point where you take action in the world giving birth to your idea.

Many ideas never reach the birth stage - they miscarry well before, as a result of being starved of the attention they need to grow. Have you ever had a brilliant idea in the middle of the night? The prospect fills you with energy and keeps you awake with a torrent of exciting possibilities and opportunities. Eventually you drop off to sleep only to awaken next morning feeling exhausted and disillusioned - in the cold light of day the idea is reduced to a total non-starter.

Yet this is no different from the oak tree's acorns that fail to sprout, returning to the earth - their potential unfulfilled. Nature's quest for quantity is a tried and tested formula that we do well to emulate. So let those ideas spring forth, give them your attention and see which take root.

The most significant questions to consider are: How does it feel? Are you excited by the vision of what could be? Does it resonate with a deeper sense of purpose? Does it attract your attention? If it does, give it the attention it demands from you freely and without qualification. Play with the possibilities in your imagination. Let them run riot in your mind on the train, in the gym, in bed. Write them down and feel the energy they evoke in you.

The process I've just outlined comes to most of us very easily, rather like playing with a pet or a child - there's fun in it. What also comes naturally will kill many of these ideas stone dead. In order to maximise their chances of survival, we need to apply two very strict disciplines. The first is to suspend our faculty of judgement so that we do not consider the ideas' worth or their practicality. The second is to prevent anyone else from doing this by keeping the idea rigorously to yourself.

A sure-fire way of terminating an idea prematurely is to expose it to the critical appraisal of others. Many of our friends, colleagues and family members have little awareness of just how fragile an early-stage idea can be and will weigh in with their opinions - with the best of intentions - blithely ignorant of the impact they can have. Fuelled by an urge to be helpful and give you the benefit of their wisdom and expertise, they can trample an idea to death in seconds. Keep your ideas to yourself until they have the strength to withstand the full blast of third-party scrutiny.

A question to avoid at this stage is how the idea will be realised. Mike Dooley, an ex PwC tax consultant, is a global speaker on the art of manifesting your dreams. He is unequivocal:

"One of the main things I speak and teach about is letting go of the 'cursed hows' and moving with your dreams. It's common that when we have a dream, we spend our time worrying about HOW we can make it a reality, when the truth is that letting go of those 'hows' is the only real way to move closer in the direction of our dreams."

This is easier said than done. Many systems of education encourage us to engage our intellects at every turn in order to work out not just how something will come into being, but all the factors that will oppose it and threaten its eventual demise.

At a personal level these include:

- I don't have the skills to do this
- Now is not the right time
- Others will do it better than I can
- I don't have the money for it

When you involve others in the consideration of your idea, you invite in their biases, blindspots and mindsets. Unless they are very much in touch with their own inner dynamics, they will project themselves onto your dream, oblivious of the simple truth that they are not you. As often as not, this will be a hatchet job, but it can also work the other way around, identifying with your vision as if it were their own, providing vicarious support and energy. Neither are helpful.

Let us deconstruct the four self-imposed barriers to progress above:

"I don't have the skills." Many skills can be learnt, but more importantly, any skill can be bought. If your idea is viable and takes root, chances are you will not be able, nor want to bring your vision to fruition on your own. You will need others. Whether you employ them or contract them, you can buy all the skills that you will need to succeed. What's more, you'll be able to partner with those that have far higher skill levels in their field of expertise than you can ever hope to develop in yourself.

Without doubt, the most effective and dynamic entrepreneurs I've worked with have admitted openly to lacking nearly all of the skills required to run their enterprise. Instead, they delegate these functions to the best people they can find, whilst they supply the vision, inspiration, energy and purpose to propel the business forward.

Paradoxically perhaps, those entrepreneurs that have a broad skill set and understanding of the operational details of running a business often get entangled in these functions to the detriment of all concerned. They also frequently fail to hire the best people to do these jobs for them, subliminally selecting those that present no threat or challenge to their abilities.

"Now is not the right time." This is a more nuanced objection which may well have some validity. It may not now be the time to resign from your job, remortgage your house, buy a company car and lease an office. But it will be the time to invest your energies in developing the idea to the point when the time is right and there is no doubt about it. There are always actions to be taken in support of your vision, regardless of circumstance.

"Others will do it better than I can." This statement exposes a significant misalignment of purpose and vision, and a compromised integrity. Take the example of a young trombone player. They love playing the trombone and they are good at it. They've been playing since they were a child and now they have the option to do it professionally. If someone were to suggest that they should rethink their career on the basis that there are others that play better than they do, it would make little sense to them. To deny doing what you love is to sabotage your life. To compare yourself with others is to break your integrity.

"I don't have the money." A favourite refrain of would-be entrepreneurs. There is a very good chance that right now, at this moment, you have enough money to take a step, however small, in pursuit of your dream. Allow some money, no matter how little, to flow towards your vision. Whether or not you believe that a universal intelligence will respond to this act of faith, you can be very sure that you will - it will feel purposeful and it will create a desire to invest more, in proportion to your means.

Will Blunt, founder of Blogger Sidekick, says: "My biggest doubter was myself. I talked myself out of starting a business for a long time—going from idea to idea, but always finding a flaw or obstacle that would keep me from just getting started. On reflection I was scared of failure and fearful of not achieving the things I dreamed about."

The Cloud of Unknowing

Once birthed into the physical world through action, the enterprise enters a very different phase of growth in which uncertainty and doubt can plague the entrepreneur. Until this point, the entrepreneurial vision was under your control, providing you kept it to yourself. Now it must encounter the full glare of the economy, stakeholders, competitors, legislation, social media and many others.

If there were any doubts about the viability of your idea before, they are now multiplied manyfold. But let's be very clear that the only doubts that can impact your enterprise are yours. No one else's misgivings can have any influence unless you adopt them and make them your own. For this reason it's important that you choose who you listen to.

Christian Mischler, cofounder and CMO of HotelQuickly says: "There are always critics and pessimists, at any stage of the business. As an entrepreneur in a competitive industry, you have to have a thick skin. It's important to listen to constructive feedback and to listen to the customer, but not get distracted by pure negativity or jealousy."

Georgina Nelson, co-founder and CEO of truRating, tells of her experience with a paid expert: "When I was just starting out, I paid a consultant to do some work on how we should get truRating to market. He was well qualified to give us the lowdown. His first slide was a running track where beyond the start line was a brick wall. He told us to stop before we had even got started. We would never make it work. His next slides were each of the Dragons in our UK TV show, Dragon's Den (Shark Tank in the US), and he made up what each of them would say to us - all along the lines of why it was officially the worst idea they had ever heard.

Kyle Gray, founder of Conversion Cake, has seen this self-sabotage very clearly and knows how to deal with it: "The biggest doubter I have ever faced is myself. I'm constantly wrestling with my own internal resistance, 'you're not working hard enough,' 'you can't do that.' The inner critic is very clever, and always knows how to adapt the same thing it is always saying to your current situation. But I have found that taking a little bit of action each day toward my goals seems to quiet this voice down."

As an entrepreneur in the midst of so many unknowns, variables and competing dynamics, it can be very tempting to blame those things outside your control for any lack of perceived success. This is where the real entrepreneur distinguishes themself from the wannabes. Only by taking full responsibility for your entire life will you find the wherewithal to navigate the challenges you meet. That is not to say you suddenly become able to exert influence on those factors previously beyond it. It does mean you use data from them to change those factors within your control.

Benny Hsu, blogger, podcaster, online entrepreneur at Get Busy Living, understands this: "At my lowest point, I would tell myself to stop waiting for a miracle. Stop hoping for your life to change. Start taking 100% responsibility for everything in your life. That means if you don't like how things are, do something about it. Take back control of your life and stop wasting your time complaining about it."

Attention and energy are focused on what you do - the process. The outcome or destination, being mutable, takes a back seat. Of course, the process is designed to manifest the vision, but the actual journey one must undertake in the application of the process to create the desired outcome is unknown.

To illustrate this uncertainty - the cloud of unknowing in which we operate - consider the circumstances of your life, including who you are, right now in its totality. Everything you have ever experienced and expressed (in thought, word and deed) has led you to this moment, here, now. You have arrived. This is it. Now consider how much of this reality you could have predicted months ago, years ago, decades ago?

The changes in you and your life are an indication of the growth or expansion that you have undergone. You could not have foreseen this expansion - if it were already known, it would be more of the same, nothing new, no uncertainty.

Telling an old friend, whom you have not seen for many years, that they have not changed one bit and are still the same old character they always were, may be intended as a compliment, yet in this light it is perhaps the greatest insult one can utter.

From our human perspectives, uncertainty is integral to the expansion we all seek. So it is mirrored in the enterprises we undertake - they are made in our image.

In the late fourteenth century AD, an anonymous author published The Cloud of Unknowing which describes how those seeking to know god will experience the cloud until they abandon everything they can think about by covering it in a cloud of forgetting.

In contemporary terms, the author is telling us that we cannot experience our essential nature (which he refers to as god) through thought. He tells us that we have to distance ourselves from thinking by forgetting it, in order to know the totality of ourselves.

The dichotomy described here - that one cannot know oneself through thought - is mirrored in the Garden of Eden myth, in which the knowledge of good and evil (a product of thought and discrimination) results in immediate expulsion from paradise.

Mindfulness, which exhorts us to live in the present, implicitly requires us to abandon thought which can only operate on data from the past.

Causation and Effectuation

In their 2018 paper, H. Øystein, P. Beate and A. Jarle wrote: "A causation approach implies that entrepreneurs focus on a predefined goal and then aim to find the means to reach this goal. An effectuation approach implies that entrepreneurs focus on the means at hand, which they aim to materialise into one or more goals that were not necessarily predefined."

An example of this would be a cook who, using causal logic, decides to cook a particular meal and then gathers the ingredients required. A cook using effectuation logic looks in the cupboard to see what is available and then creates a meal from whatever is found.

Causation is frequently the orthodox, often assumed approach to entrepreneurial activity whereby we set a vision of our chosen outcome and use it to determine the means with which we will achieve it. The modus operandi, tools, processes, people and place are all selected in support of our holy grail. In extremis, the end justifies the means.

Effectuation takes a more pragmatic approach, allowing the available means to modulate the end. The five principles of effectuation, devised by Professor Saras Sarasvathy, serve to illustrate the differences between these two entrepreneurial paths:

The Bird in Hand Principle: Start with your means. Don't wait for the perfect opportunity. Start taking action, based on what you have readily available: who you are, what you know, and who you know.

The Affordable Loss Principle: - Set an affordable loss and evaluate opportunities based on whether the downside is acceptable, rather than on the attractiveness of the predicted upside.

The Lemonade Principle: Leverage contingencies and embrace surprises that arise from uncertain situations, remaining flexible rather than tethered to existing goals.

The Crazy-Quilt Principle: Form partnerships with people and organisations willing to make a real commitment to jointly creating the future with you. Don't worry so much about competitive analysis and strategic planning.

The Pilot in the Plane Principle: Control the controllable. Of course not everything can be shaped or controlled, but effectuation encourages you, as the pilot of your venture, to focus on those aspects of the environment which are, at least to a certain degree, within your control.

Effectuation is the practical response to one's circumstances, but does it violate one's vision? Is it purely an expedient that runs the risk of undermining the integrity of one's dreams?

I would argue that your vision can be anything - expedient or not - providing it aligns with your sense of purpose and the integrity of that purpose. It is that inner urge to express oneself, through action, that needs to be held sacrosanct, not the means through which one does it. So the question is not so much about the nature of the entrepreneur's vision, as whether or not it provides a vehicle for them to express their sense of purpose.

Many of us feel a need to exchange knowledge with others - a laudable purpose. The ways in which we do that cover a wide spectrum - from sharing an experience with a friend to building an online learning platform - from primary school teaching to authoring books. The purpose is one, the means are many.

The Corruption of Purpose

When vision is aligned with purpose, and the purpose is pure and impeccable, success is all but guaranteed. But when the integrity of one's purpose is corrupted by external factors, trouble ensues.

Elizabeth Holmes' vision to build a better way of diagnosing disease was unimpeachable. But was her purpose really to help create a healthier world? Or had her purpose become corrupted by her idolisation of Steve Jobs? Did creating a veneer of success become more important to her than confronting the irresolvable technical problems she met?

When your true, inner point of reference becomes supplanted by an external one, integrity is compromised. This is why hero-worship and role-modelling, beyond one's teenage years, is fraught with risk. When we observe someone else - anyone else - we see only a facade of behaviours and accumulations. We see nothing of the internal dynamics, the thoughts, feelings and perspectives that they live, and we know nothing of the journey that they are on.

The bare fact is: you can only be you with integrity. Diluting that alignment with yourself renders you incomplete - unwholesome.

Be your own hero, be your own role-model and be guided by the way you feel, not by others' opinions and behaviours..

So how do you stay on course? How do you navigate the vicissitudes of business, adjusting your vision without losing alignment to purpose? Ultimately, the only question you have to ask yourself is: How does it feel? The feeling will tell you everything you need to know.

Some years ago I was running a small business on an interim basis. I had made some very positive changes, operationally and culturally, and wanted to expand the business through acquisition. I could feel a lack of appetite for this strategy from the owners, but more importantly, I was not feeling much enthusiasm for it myself. Looking back, what kept me going was the belief that not only was it expected of me, but that it would be the course of action that any interim manager, worth their salt, would take. My integrity compromised by considerations of what others would think, the vision failed to get any traction and rapidly came to an abrupt halt, as did my job!

Regrettably, all too often, our innermost feelings are drowned out by our noisy minds, over-active intellects and ambitious egos, desperately seeking a rationale that we can latch on to. The problem with logic and reason is that they only operate on historic data, whereas feelings exist exclusively in the here and now.

A sustainable feeling of success comes from following what interests and excites you, taking action to realise it with no focus on the final outcome and the resolve to keep going.

Takeaways

- Success is a feeling now, not a future result
- Entrepreneur and Enterprise need to develop together
- New ideas initially need nurturing and protection from 3rd party judgement
- Prioritise the What, over the How
- Feel your way forward, whatever you think
- Honour what excites and inspires you

PRACTICAL INTEGRATION

This final chapter provides the keys to putting all that has been previously explored into practice and optimising your chances of experiencing entrepreneurial success, whatever that means to you and however it appears to the world.

It should be abundantly clear by now that this approach focuses on adjustments to our inner worlds of thinking and feeling as levers for changing our experience of our outer world. So a dearth of detailed entrepreneurial strategic, operational and financial advice should come as no surprise.

The word practical in the chapter title suggests action, but the action I exhort you to take is inner action, the impact of which may not be immediately visible in the outer world. This kind of action is just as practical as running a social media campaign or taking a shower. In fact, as we explored earlier on, thoughts are causal and therefore more 'real' than deeds.

The word integration signifies making whole or complete. It is the process of achieving integrity in terms of being everything that you are and excluding nothing from it.

There are three inner dimensions of leadership which need to be established as a foundation for any enterprise. They are Integrity, Purpose and Resilience.

Without integrity, as Elizabeth Holmes demonstrated, the enterprise can give every semblance of growth and success whilst rotting at the core and ultimately falling apart.

Without purpose, an entrepreneur will never channel the energy and vision required to inspire others to support the enterprise.

Without resilience, the entrepreneur will fail to jump the hurdles they will inevitably find on their journey.

All three need to be embedded to some degree in the entrepreneur's approach to give them any chance of success.

There are also three outer dimensions of leadership which are central to success. They are Vision, Culture and Delegation.

Without a communicable and relatable vision, the entrepreneur cannot engage and inspire others to join them on their journey.

Without a positive and supportive culture - collective behaviour - the entrepreneur will fail to retain those who know they have a choice and refuse to sacrifice their own well-being.

Without true delegation, the enterprise cannot grow - neither can anyone within it.

But before we consider how to enact these aspects of leadership, let's explore the fundamentals of success in terms of what it means for you and me:

The somewhat hackneyed but common ideal of entrepreneurial success is the accrual of wealth - the making of money. Money is a wonderful thing which facilitates many of the experiences we desire from our time on earth. Of course, the money itself has no use or value until it is spent - it is no more than a medium of exchange - so the more astute realise that it is the fruits of money that we desire and that a yearning for the money itself can only be a perversion of this desire.

Perhaps this is where the idea that 'the love of money is the root of all evil' derives from. But money itself is neutral, being no more the source of evil than that of good.

Yet on closer inspection, it is not even what money buys that constitutes real success. We've all noticed how the initial euphoria of a new house, a new car, a new wardrobe, will fade leaving you wanting more. No matter what we accrue, the emotions subside leaving us, more or less, with the same feelings as before, plus a little disappointment thrown in.

As we repeat this cycle of frustration, we may begin to realise that it is not even the possessions and experiences that give us what we want - let alone the money that buys them - but the feelings themselves.

FEELING GOOD

What we really want is to feel good - happy, content, peaceful, enthusiastic and whole.

Life is a felt experience and everything we do is intended to make us feel better - no exceptions. All decisions are feeling-based, regardless of whatever rational analysis may have preceded them. Even altruistic, charitable and philanthropic acts are driven by the feeling payback they provide us with.

By taking responsibility for our feelings - and refusing to attribute them to anything outside of us - we can create the world we want to live in and experience the success that is available to us all. This is real power.

In other words, if you don't like the way you feel, change it! Think differently. This is an injunction that is far too simple for our sophisticated intellects to make easy.

As we start to establish the feelings we want to experience - independently of the circumstances we find ourselves in - we quite naturally attract new, beneficial circumstances that resonate with how we feel. We see so many more opportunities with our heads held high, full of energy and clarity, than we ever can weighed down by concern, unease and depression. Being able to determine the way you feel is the only success worth having and brings everything else we desire in its train.

Taking responsibility for the way we feel runs against much

of what our parents, our schools and society tells us. It is a radical contradiction of the received wisdom. In the eyes of many, it is an outrageous indictment of our human right to be offended by those that behave in any way that we deem undesirable.

But blame is judgement and, as the book of Genesis would have us believe, judgement - knowledge of good and evil - leads to summary expulsion from paradise, the ultimate place of feeling good.

Establishing sovereignty over your feelings is to reclaim power. No longer are you at the mercy of other people's behaviour, you begin to feel as you would wish to feel. And in feeling good about yourself, those around you and your circumstances, you become receptive to those opportunities, situations and relationships that support those feelings.

This is, of course, the essential message of the law of attraction. If you are naturally sceptical of new-age fads, you can rest assured that this is nothing remotely new. References to it can be found in many metaphysical and philosophical teachings going back millennia.

This law can be seen operating at many levels of creation - from the attraction of gravity holding our solar system in place, to the bringing of like-minded people together. At a personal level it dictates that whatever you hold in mind as a thought/feeling, more of the same will be added. If the focus of attention is haphazard, so will be our experience of life.

You don't even have to buy into any metaphysical beliefs for this to work. Your elevated, conscious, clear and satisfied state of mind will predispose you to identifying those things that will give you more of the same. The reverse is also true.

So the formula for elevating your feelings is to recognise when you experience negative feelings (which is easy, because they feel uncomfortable) and to refocus on thoughts that create good feelings.

It's important to recognise that this action of mind does not deny reality, but it does circumvent the judgement of it, a critical distinction. The trick is to play with it and see what happens.

Getting What You Want

Frequently, when thinking of something you want, you'll be feeling its lack. So you get more of that. The attraction is inclusive - it does not exclude - so whatever your focus of attention is, more will be provided. And rather like gravity will attract any mass, so will this law attract whatever your thought/feeling focus is - regardless whether you deem it good, bad or neutral. Qualification - a form of judgement - is a human artifice which is not recognised by this law.

So if you find yourself perpetually frustrated by a lack of 'success' in any realm, ask yourself whether you are focussed on what you want or, instead, the lack of it. You can easily tell which, by the way they feel. If you feel frustration, you are dwelling on lack and will likely attract more. If you feel a joyful, hopeful expectancy, or similar positive and pleasant feelings, you will experience more and more evidence of what pleases you in your life. It must be.

Indeed you will experience an abundance of whatever you focus your attention on - even if it is an abundance of lack!

A common objection to this approach is that it is a denial of reality. Faced with an empty bank account, you are pretending to be affluent. This is indeed how it looks from a perspective of lack. However, if you perceive the wealth and abundance that you do have - the food on your table, the house you live in, the friends and family you love, the water you drink, the air you breathe, the good health you enjoy, the nature you appreciate - you cannot fail but to start experiencing good feelings, based on a much more profound perception of reality. At the very least, this better state of mind will inspire and enable you to respond much more effectively to whatever circumstance you find yourself in and whatever you are moved to change.

A critical aspect of getting what you want is a ruthless honesty with yourself that it is what you *really* want, as opposed to a craving that is coming from a place other than integrity. As I write, the US presidential election features two men, both of whom are having to disregard serious questions of probity and health, in order to win the race. It is not clear to this impartial bystander that either are putting their country first.

To have integrity is to be complete and whole within oneself. One of the favourite ways we compromise our integrity is by using external points of reference to guide us, rather than our own, internal navigational system. So your course of action may be to please someone else, whilst neglecting your own or your business's needs. In a professional environment, this often takes the form of failing to address an issue to avoid consequences that you would rather dodge. The underperforming employee goes unchallenged in order to circumvent possible confrontation.

Your internal navigation system presents the feelings you feel in respect of any thought that you give your attention to. Every thought has an attendant feeling which allows you to assess how in tune it is with you. When a thought produces an unpleasant feeling, it is telling you that it is not resonant with who you are, and thus gives you the opportunity to move your attention away on to something that does resonate.

Your integrity is reinforced through your pursuit of good-feeling thoughts and compromised by allowing your attention to be drawn and held by thoughts that create disagreeable feelings. Clearly, this system is wholly personal to you and needs no input other than the thoughts you are thinking and the reality you are experiencing. Your job is to be as tuned-in to, and mindful of your feelings as you can be - from moment to moment.

WHAT'S YOUR PURPOSE?

The purpose of life is to live - to experience life, to expand through it and to express into it. But what is your individual purpose - how do you express through your particular circumstances, preferences and aspirations? Chances are you are already doing it to some extent. The question is: how does it feel? Does what you do fill you with joy, satisfaction and meaning? Or does it leave you dissatisfied and hankering for something other?

Once more, your feelings - and only your feelings - can guide you to that better feeling place where you find a greater sense of purpose.

Here is a simple way of tuning in to those feelings through reflecting on the following questions:

When you are physically idle (not concerned with doing anything) what do you tend to think about? Do you daydream about things - if so, what?

What do you tend to do when time and space allows? What activity do you gravitate towards, other than general relaxation like watching TV or using Social Media?

What used to excite you as a child? Think back to the activities that you loved when you were young.

Do you have any unfulfilled ambitions? Things that you want to achieve that you've had to neglect because of practical considerations?

Think back over your life and identify those things that you've been particularly good at, even though they may seem unimportant or of little value.

Imagine that all the responsibilities that seem to restrict your time suddenly disappeared. What would you do with your new-found time and freedom?

Imagine that you have a very large bank balance - far, far more than you need to live, as you do, for the rest of your life. How would you use it?

See if you can sense any urge to pursue something that, as yet, remains under-fulfilled. Don't get caught up in projects and careers - we'll get to those shortly. Instead get a feeling for the kinds of action that, when you imagine them, give you a feeling of excitement and anticipation. Don't let practicalities, or any consideration of other people get in the way… for now.

As previously mentioned, the word purpose derives from old French meaning: what you put out. It is what you express through your life. It could be caring for others, making music, fixing things, designing things, communicating ideas, being with animals, cleaning, fighting, teaching - the list is endless.

The way to maintain and invigorate your sense of purpose is, having identified it, or possibly more than one, simply to do more of what aligns with it and less of what doesn't!

Working, living or playing 'on purpose' feels good and satisfies every dimension of being. Activities that are rooted purely in pleasing others, survival, security and habit cannot. Of course, some of these activities may be non-negotiable, but our job is to build on what feels purposeful and begin to move away from what doesn't.

What can you do more of and less of?

BOUNCING BACK

Resilience is the ability to bounce back - to restore your mental and emotional equilibrium after it has been perturbed. In the context of inner action, it is the ability to maintain or refocus your attention on your desired goal, independently of external factors. It is also the ability to maintain your attention on those thoughts that cultivate the most positive feelings for you to experience.

Resilience requires you to be present - to be constantly alert to how you feel and to make appropriate adjustments as necessary. It is not so much about controlling your mind as making a conscious choice of those thoughts you give your energy to and the feelings they evoke.

Having possibly spent much of your life allowing your mind the freedom to go with whatever thoughts are running, regardless of the qualities they exhibit and the feelings they generate, changing this habit of mind is rarely an overnight task. But with just a little bit of persistence, you will see results in days and weeks, rather than months and years.

Your attention is life-giving. Look back on your life to identify those things you have kept your focus on and see how they have flourished. You will likely notice patterns of things you realised - made real - whether they were wanted or not, You simply got more of whatever you gave life to through your attention. Resilience is achieved through maintaining your attention on those things you want, whilst withholding it from anything you don't want.

•

So far in this chapter, we've examined the true nature of success and how the use of your mind is the determining factor. This holds true regardless of what action we take, since all words and deeds emanate from our thoughts and feelings. Thoughts are more real than things.

We've also discussed how this plays out into your clarity of purpose, your integrity and your resilience. Now we explore how these inner qualities play out into the entrepreneurial world through vision, culture and delegation.

INSPIRING OTHERS

Having established the three personal foundations of Purpose, Integrity and Resilience, it now remains to externalise these in order to realise your dreams in the world of form.

The entrepreneur does this through Vision, Culture and Delegation. These are the three corporate foundations of the enterprise. They deliver both the inspiration and the direction to get the right things done in support of the dream.

Clarity of purpose will eventually urge you to take action in order to express your purpose out in the world. This happens through vision - otherwise known as a dream, an aspiration, an ambition - whatever you want to call it. Its quality is that it is unmanifest - it does not yet exist in the world of form as you envisage it.

Vision is a picture of the future, yet to be realised as an expression of your purpose. Your purpose can express in many ways: if your purpose is to fight - if you are drawn to physical confrontation - at one end of the scale, you could be attracted to performing historical reenactments of famous local battles and decide to create a society for this purpose. Alternatively, your urge to fight could manifest as a vision of being a champion boxer in your weight division. Less legitimately, you might even harbour ambitions of being top dog in your local street gang.

You can express your sense of purpose in myriad ways, so how do you select which one to go with? As we explored, this choice is made according to feeling: which possibility feels best. However, whereas your purpose is independent of circumstance, your vision needs to take practicalities into account. So do your due diligence. Research everything relevant. Go where your curiosity and interest take you. Follow the inspiration. Draw from the five principles of effectuation without being constrained by them. Then, once you have exhausted this work to your satisfaction, forget everything you have learnt and let your feelings guide you.

Remember that your vision is a plastic thought-form of your purpose. It can be changed or replaced at any time. Your purpose, in contrast, is likely to remain less mutable. Some entrepreneurs pride themselves on manifesting their vision, unchanged. Others celebrate how they navigated circumstances to create an enterprise that no one would have foreseen, least of all the entrepreneurs themselves.

If your vision is congruent with your inner sense of purpose, it cannot but inspire you. Inspiring you, it will inspire others and draw the right people to you.

•

Culture also attracts those that resonate with it. The word *thrive* derives from the Old Norsk meaning to grasp to oneself. A thriving culture is one that attracts people to it - inclusive, not exclusive. Culture is collective behaviour: the way an organisation responds to an event. Often, the cultural ideal held by the leadership does not reflect in the organisation's response - they are misaligned and so the reality lacks integrity. Many of us have been disillusioned weeks after starting a new job, discovering that the culture we were led to believe in, was a far cry from the reality. The Broken CEO presents several examples of this mismatch.

Given that culture is essentially behaviour, and that the individual with the most influence is the leader, it is not a stretch to suggest that the entrepreneur has more impact on culture than any other single factor. In other words, how the entrepreneur behaves will largely determine the culture of the enterprise. Objectors to this statement will often cite how pockets of malign culture can often take root within a very positive and supportive one. This is always explained in terms of action (behaviour) that the leader neglects - for whatever reason - to take. Behaviour that does not align to the culture you want needs to be challenged and resolved just as the behaviour you want to encourage needs your support.

It is not enough to praise positive behaviour, it is incumbent on the leader to arrest negative behaviour. John Stuart Mill said in 1867: "Bad men need nothing more to compass their ends, than that good men should look on and do nothing."

Unchecked, rogue managers can progressively establish their own fiefdoms, facilitated by a leader that turns a blind eye to keep the peace and avoid confrontation. In each case that I've been involved in, resolving the situation was more like amputating a limb than lancing a boil.

The more tuned-in to your own behaviour, and the more consistent it is with your integrity, the more impact and influence it will have on those around you. This will attract those it appeals to and repel those that are not in alignment with it.

•

Delegation is the release of task and responsibility to others - it is the ultimate expression of activity within an enterprise. Growth can only take place through delegation. Yet the imperative here is not organisational growth, it is personal growth. So many enterprises fail to reach potential because organisational growth - generally trumpeted through key performance indicators (KPIs) - is promoted at the expense of the growth of individuals within it. Just as thought is causal to deed, so is personal growth to the performance of the enterprise.

It is often said that if you can't measure something, you can't manage it. I've found this piece of received wisdom to be diametrically opposed to the truth. Those things that cannot be measured seem often, if not always, to be the causes of those things that can, and therefore worthy of far more scrutiny.

I have encountered many cases of entrepreneurs unknowingly restricting the growth of their enterprise through a lack of self-knowledge and an inability to shift their perspective - their fixation on KPIs drowning out any consideration of what is in the best interests of their people, individually and collectively. Nowhere does this manifest more strongly than in the act of delegation. When a founder ruthlessly prioritises performance, they will inevitably circumvent delegation which has both an overhead and a risk attached. The overhead is the communication and training that may be involved - the risk is that of the delegate failing to execute optimally. Fuelled by the notion that 'If you want something done, do it yourself', the entrepreneur resolutely refuses to fully release the task to a delegate.

Even more frequent and insidious is the delegation of a task without the responsibility that would accompany it. Delegation requires the surrender of both task and responsibility, without which the micromanager turns a task for one into an activity for two. In this instance, personal growth suffers needlessly, whilst the impact on the productivity KPI hopefully needs no explanation.

Let's now summarise the formula for entrepreneurial success:

- Take responsibility for your feelings - choose your thoughts
- Focus on what you want, relentlessly, and *feel* the impact
- Maintain integrity by referencing your inner guidance
- Clarify your purpose - let it inform your activity
- Develop resilience - keep the inner focus independent of the outer world
- Create your vision in alignment with your sense of purpose
- Establish the culture you want by living it yourself
- Delegate task and responsibility for personal and organisational growth

These eight imperatives will guide you to a more expansive entrepreneurial journey and transform that sense of struggle - pushing, shoving, grasping, craving and effort - into one of an exciting and exuberant flow where expected and unexpected people, circumstances and events make life the fascinating, wondrous and deeply fulfilling experience it can be for us all.

Last Words

I hope to have made the point in preceding chapters that entrepreneurialism is simply the act of transforming a thought into a thing - an idea into form.

This process is essentially the raison d'être of humanity in its quest to experience, expand and express itself. The act is deceptively simple: imagine, feel and do. Yet we get in the way at every step, struggling with judgements, doubts, fear, conflict - all of which, contrary to appearances, are of our own making.

The real work to be done is to get out of our own way, let go and allow how we feel to guide us at every step of the journey. A sense of purpose provides the fuel just as long as our vision remains in alignment with it.

When we remain faithful to the process, any sense of struggle simply dematerialises not unlike a dream on waking. Success is *felt* - independently of results - and manifests as fulfilment, joy and harmony, in the moment - now - not in some future that may be but never is.

It is not so much the business of transmuting struggle into flow, as elevating oneself into a dimension in which struggle ceases to exist... and never really did.

We can now further summarise all that we have so far unfolded in five simple rules. Like much of the guidance in this book, these are not new or unique. They are modern echoes of perennial wisdom that have stood the test of time and practice.

If you take nothing else from this book, these will more than suffice to lead you to success - not limited to the conventional meaning of the word - in whatever enterprise you choose to realise:

1. Follow what excites and inspires you right now and as often as you can.

2. Do what inspires you to the best of your ability and take it as far as you can go.

3. Act on your passion with no expectation of what the outcome should be. Do it for the love of it.

4. Keep going and navigate the difficulties. Learn from them and grow. Choose to stay positive regardless.

5. Constantly investigate your belief systems and release those beliefs not consistent with who you prefer to be.

APPENDICES

Appendix 1 - Meditation

Meditation is a widely misunderstood practice. Strictly speaking, it's not even a practice, more a state of mind. Perhaps the reason meditation is so misunderstood is that we try to understand it intellectually when it operates outside our intellects. What that means is there is no point thinking about it. Thinking about meditation is not meditating! The good part of that is that you can't fail at at it - you either do it… or you don't.

Like many things, the proof is in the pudding. Does meditating change you, your relationships, your life? My answer to that is an unequivocal *yes!* My experience, and that of my clients, to whom I introduce it, is that meditation makes for a calmer, clearer existence, in which stress has less impact, relationships become more harmonious and the ups and downs of the world around us affect us less. The desperation to achieve abates and we enjoy inactivity as much as activity.

But my experience is mine, not yours. So instead of concerning yourself with how it works, if it will work or why it works, I suggest you try it. 3rd party proof, statistics and scientific studies on the effects of meditation are just intellectual noise, which can easily delay your own experience.

So this is how you start:

Time of Day

The best time is first thing in the morning, before breakfast - ideally before sunrise, though that can be challenging in some latitudes. Children can also make this time impractical. If you can't meditate in the morning, the evening works well too. You may have to experiment to find your best time. Meditating during the day can be problematic, not just from a practical point of view, but energetically - we are not as well disposed to sitting still. However meditating at any time is preferable to not meditating at all.

Duration

Some first-time meditators have difficulty with more than a couple of minutes. Others settle into 10 or 20 minutes without a problem. The important thing is to go with whatever works for you. Daily practice is the initial goal - practising everyday or as frequently as possible. Better to meditate for two minutes everyday for a week, than 30 minutes on a Sunday. See how long is comfortable and establish it as a daily practice for a month. Then start to gently increment it up to 20 minutes a day. Use a gentle alarm so you don't have to check the time.

Things to avoid

Don't practice after eating, or drinking alcohol. If you're feeling very emotional or very tired, skip the practice - there's always tomorrow. If you are undergoing any mental health treatment, check with your therapist or doctor before you start meditating. Finally, if you experience any significant levels of anxiety during meditation, stop and come back to it another time.

Environment

Quiet surroundings are generally helpful to establishing a meditation practice, but if you can't find quiet, don't let that stop you. Try to use the same place every day if you can - this is part of creating a helpful habit to support the practice against the many reasons we can all find for not doing it. Use an upright chair - the kind you might have at a dinner table, or in your kitchen.

Posture

Sit with your spine straight, away from the back of the chair and your feet flat on the floor. Keep your head level, neither up nor down. Put your hands on your legs or in your lap. Close your eyes.

Practice

Focus your attention on your breath going in and out of your nose. If your nose is blocked, breathe through your mouth! Be aware of the air flowing in and out of you. If you are breathing through your nose, let the attention settle at the bridge, between the eyes and feel the breath flowing there. That's all you do: be aware of the breath flowing in and out.

Distractions

Sooner or later a thought will intrude: "Am I doing this right? Is it working? What am I meant to be feeling? Where is the transcendental experience? What shall I have for lunch? I need to scratch an itch. How long do I have left? What time is it? I need to look at my bank balance when I've finished. I wonder if my mother will phone tonight" etc. etc. etc. There is no end to the thinking.

You will not stop the thinking - don't even try. Just come back to the point of attention. By trying to stop the thinking, you will just create more. The mind is meant to think, just like the heart is meant to pump. You will find that as you maintain focus on the breath, both your heart and your thinking will slow, but without any help from you!

Whether you find that your meditation is very chaotic - full of thoughts, feelings and distractions - or very serene, calm and peaceful, it doesn't matter. That may sound strange but remember that our intellects are dead set on making everything good or bad. In truth meditation is neither. It cannot fail. The only failure is not practising. Also remember that it is operating *under the radar* - subconsciously - so don't judge it.

Afterwards

It is very common to feel a sense of tranquillity, ease and well-being after meditating - though as I said above, it doesn't matter if you don't. When you do, keep it with you and don't let it dissipate too easily. Maintaining that sense of presence and serenity is the basis of mindfulness, another good practice to explore and establish. Though be mindful that much of what has been written about mindfulness is commercially motivated and not always accurate.

Pause regularly during the day and immerse yourself in that feeling of peace for a few seconds.

Long term

Once you've established a practice, you'll probably be drawn to learning more about meditation. Beware that meditation is a long-term business - it's a lifetime practice - so the real authorities on meditation will have experience measured in decades, not months or even years. Meditation has religious and spiritual connotations which put many people off taking it up. The truth is that meditation is not a religious practice, although many religions promote meditation or practices, which appear similar. Meditation does not require any belief other than in your own existence and experience. In this respect, atheists and devout believers are very similar - they both believe in something, which is not necessarily known and experienced: the believer in a deity; the atheist in the impossibility of a deity. The agnostic, on the other hand, admits to not knowing.

Whatever your belief-system, investigate what you are drawn to, being aware of the resonance it has with your deepest being. Only you will know which path to follow. Moderation is a good thing - try what you are drawn to but don't flit from one thing to another like a butterfly - give each experiment time, or stick with what works for you.

Resources

The style of meditation that suits you may well be different from mine - it's a very personal choice. Here are a few resources, which may be of value to you:

The *Transcendental Meditation* technique or TM is a form of silent mantra meditation, developed by Maharishi Mahesh Yogi.

The *School of Meditation* is 57 years old and has taught meditation to thousands of people. It's a non-profit, registered charity based in London but also has branches around the UK

The *London Buddhist Centre* teaches meditation and Buddhism in a way that is relevant to modern London life. It is a public centre, open to all, with no expectation of Buddhist involvement.

APPENDIX 2 - PROGRAMS

You'll find some of the changes to your leadership, which are detailed in this book, straightforward. Sometimes we're so ready for change, just a small nudge will make it happen. I have experienced many times over how the best advice comes as confirmation of what we already know, but may not have actioned.

Other behavioural shifts need a little more time, energy and persistence. The programs outlined below provide a blend of weekly, online material, supported by regular 1-on-1 meetings, to support sustainable change. The material covers much of the contents of this book, and more. The meetings provide an opportunity to explore how the material relates specifically to you and your live work challenges. The combination is a powerful catalyst for transformation.

LEAD Program

The Leadership Evolution and Accelerated Development program comprises 3 modules corresponding to parts 2,3 and 4 of this book:

- Personal Evolution - explores your mental and emotional dynamics and their impact on your life

- Relationship Evolution - applies the personal insights to your relationships with others

- Leadership Evolution - embeds the personal and relationship shifts into your leadership of others.

The program delivers 24 weeks of material supported by nine 1-on-1 meetings.

Personal Evolution Program

This equates to the first module of the LEAD program, which focuses on your inner, mental and emotional dynamics and unfolds over 8 weeks with 4 x 1-on-1 meetings.

Management Evolution Program

A bespoke, 8 week program designed specifically for your needs and challenges as a senior manager, comprising weekly, online material and 4 x 1-on-1 meetings.

Senior Team Evolution Program

An 8 week program for teams of up to 12 senior managers which deliver weekly material, group meetings and 1-on-1 meeting for optimal impact on collective leadership.

•

Client feedback

"I would absolutely recommend the LEAD Program for the experienced professional who needs to take time to reflect and push on to the next level." Nick F - HRD

"The following 6 months changed not only my methods at work but some of the driving thoughts deep within too. The bonus being how much it helped me beyond work, at home and personally." Chris L - FD

"I now feel much more in control of my life, worry a lot less and can properly switch off, which I struggled with massively before." - Graeme H - CEO

For more information email: lead@chrispearse.co.uk

APPENDIX 3 - RESOURCES

Here are some of my online resources which provide more perspective on the very broad subject of leadership:

>linkedin.com/in/chrispearse1/

>forbes.com/sites/chrispearse/

>chrispearse.co.uk/

The books listed below have been important influences on the writing of this book:

>Emotional Intelligence - Daniel Goleman

>Navigating Complexity - Arthur Battram

>Autobiography of a Yogi - Paramahamsa Yogananda

>The Republic - Plato

>Inner Engineering - Sadhguru

>Tao Te Ching - Lao Tsu

>Supercoach - Michael Neill

ABOUT THE AUTHOR

I initially discovered my outer purpose at around 8 years old, when I developed an insatiable appetite for taking things apart. Anything from alarm clocks and radios to bicycles and lawnmowers. My parents often provided the right incentive for putting them back together again, affording even more learning.

Engineering was on the cards as a career, until I fell in love with chemistry, building a makeshift laboratory in the garage. I was besotted with the appearance of different chemicals, their smell, the way they reacted together and the colours they gave to flames. I loved the glassware, the retorts, beakers and test tubes. Chemistry became my new fixation… until I blew myself up in a silly experiment. I should have known better.

On completing a degree in electrical and electronic engineering, I threw myself into designing the hardware and software to control a variety of applications from networking computers, to digital effects for film and TV.

At around 30 I began to feel a different calling - one that involved technology *and* people. Within a year I found myself working abroad having set up a new business, selling and marketing technology across southern Europe. A number of commercial roles followed culminating in a leadership role with a global remit.

Looking back on this period I see clearly that it was instrumental in teaching me how organisations and the people within them worked. The same curiosity I had as an 8 year old was alive and well. But the real game changer for me was understanding that our behaviour as human beings follows a completely different set of rules from that of the mechanical, chemical and electronic systems I loved.

I studied personal development, psychology, metaphysics, yoga, organisational development, coaching and leadership, meeting many remarkable minds en route. I balanced my learning of the outer world with insights into my inner world through reflection, contemplation and meditation. Far from being incompatible, as I had feared, they quickly became integrated - I could no longer make sense of the world of people and organisations without reference to my own inner world. The hermetic expression, As Above, So Below, showed the way.

Soon I was working with leaders, directors and senior managers of many different shapes and sizes of organisation - multinationals, bluechips, government, universities, charities, and small businesses. I found the same dynamics at play in all of them. All of them subject to many of the symptoms and causes explored in this book. All of them potentially able to change for the better through looking inward, as well as outward.

Since publishing The Broken CEO, my sense of a vast intelligence at play (literally!) in the orchestration and maintenance of every dimension of life deepens daily. Logically, one might expect this to be accompanied by a sense of restrictive predetermination but paradoxically the reverse is true: freedom and free will seem to flourish instead.

In occasional flashes of insight it would seem that there really is nothing to do other than witness the expansion and flow of life - which includes our thoughts, feelings, decisions and actions. Or in the words of the Dao:

When nothing is done, nothing is left undone.

And so all struggle, adversity and effort simply vanish from our experience.

ALSO…

If you liked this book, please take the time to review it on Amazon.

PLUS…

Send a link or a screenshot of a review that you've written about this book to:

chris@chrispearse.co.uk

and we will send you a link to our Leadership Scorecard which will reveal your opportunities for development as a leader.

This is a qualitative indication of the potential impact that Leadership Development can have on your capacity to lead yourself, your people and your organisation.

You can also invite your senior team to complete the Scorecard.

Printed in Great Britain
by Amazon